# Beyond the Piggy Bank
## TO EARLY FINANCIAL INDEPENDENCE

Todd W. Manning

**All Rights Reserved:**
Copyright © 2013, 2014, 2015 by Todd W. Manning

First Published Print Edition: 2015
ISBN: 0990451127
ISBN-13: 9780990451129
Library of Congress Control Number: 2015915274
Todd W Manning, Westfield, NJ

No part of this book may be reproduced, stored or transmitted in any form or by any means, electronic or mechanical, including photocopying, recording or by any information storage or retrieval systems, without prior permission in writing from the author.

Cover: Designed by Austin Rubben (austinrubben@yahoo.com); Exclusive ownership rights transferred/granted to Todd W. Manning on May 22, 2014 by way of a fully executed, legally binding agreement.

**Disclaimer:**

The views expressed herein are my personal opinions and do not necessarily represent those of my past, present or future employers and or their subsidiaries, partners, employees, contractors or consultants. This writing is exclusively my own work product and does not represent the positions, strategies or opinions of any organization I have ever been or may be employed by or for. This disclaimer also broadly applies to my spouse's opinions and her past, present and future employers.

**Dedication:** *This labor of love is fondly dedicated to my two wonderful sons, Douglas and Tyler, who bring me much joy and inspire me to reach new parenting heights ... And, to my uniquely special nieces and nephews, Kimberly, Malissa, Michael, Arabella and Christopher, whom I also care so deeply about.*

# Table of Contents

Acknowledgements · · · · · · · · · · · · · · · · · · · · · · · · · · · · · · · · · · · · · · · xi
Message to My Children · · · · · · · · · · · · · · · · · · · · · · · · · · · · · · · · · · xiii
Preface · · · · · · · · · · · · · · · · · · · · · · · · · · · · · · · · · · · · · · · · · · · · · · · · · · xv
Introduction · · · · · · · · · · · · · · · · · · · · · · · · · · · · · · · · · · · · · · · · · · · · · xvii
What this saving guide IS: · · · · · · · · · · · · · · · · · · · · · · · · · · · · · · · · xviii
What this saving guide is NOT: · · · · · · · · · · · · · · · · · · · · · · · · · · · · ·xix

Phase I    The Early Stages, Laying a Solid Foundation:
           (Your Teenage Years & Beyond – Working on the Basics) · · · · · · · · · · · 1

Chapter 1  Education/Career · · · · · · · · · · · · · · · · · · · · · · · · · · · · · · · · · · · · · · 3
           A. Up to Secondary School (Through High School) · · · · · · · · · · · · · · · 4
           B. Post-Secondary School (College & Graduate Studies) · · · · · · · · · · · 5
           C. Important Career Factors - Industry, On-Going
           Training & Balance · · · · · · · · · · · · · · · · · · · · · · · · · · · · · · · · · · · · · · · 9
           D. Miscellaneous Considerations for Full Time
           Students · · · · · · · · · · · · · · · · · · · · · · · · · · · · · · · · · · · · · · · · · · · · · · · 13

Chapter 2  Health (Mental & Physical) · · · · · · · · · · · · · · · · · · · · · · · · · · · · · 15
           A. Making Intelligent Food Consumption Decisions · · · · · · · · · · · 17
           B. Developing a Sound Mind Through Healthy Lifestyle Choices · · · · 19
           C. Establishing a Regular Physical Exercise Routine · · · · · · · · · · · · · 22

Chapter 3  Investment Vehicles · · · · · · · · · · · · · · · · · · · · · · · · · · · · · · · · · · · 24
           A. The Importance of Prudent Investing · · · · · · · · · · · · · · · · · · · · · 25
           B. "Risk Free" Investing - Essential in Your Early Years · · · · · · · · · · 26
           C. Riskier Investing – When You Can Afford to Lose! · · · · · · · · · · · · 30

           D. Key Investment Principles to Accelerate EFI ················33
           E. False Investments (Fool's Gold) ···························36

Phase II    The Middle Stages – Establishing a Sturdy Frame:
               (Early Adulthood/ New Found Independence -
               Managing the Necessities) ·································40

Chapter 4  Food/Essentials ·············································42
           A. Brand Disloyalty ·······································43
           B. 7 Ways to Save········································43
           C. Spend More On Healthier Food Choices - ················51
           D. Safer Non-Food Essentials·······························52

Chapter 5  Housing ·····················································54
           A. Renting – A Reasonable First Step·······················55
           B. Owning - Often a Highly Desirable Second Step ·········56
           C. Living Below Your Home Ownership Means By: ·········58
           D. 3 Essentials to Look For in a Home ·····················61
           E. Starter Homes··········································64
           F. Fixer-Uppers ···········································65
           G. Conflicting Role of Real Estate Agents ···················66
           H. Basements – A "Near Essential" in Some Places··········67
           I. Importance of Attractive Landscaping ····················68
           J. Saving on Furnishings ···································70
           K. Reap Additional Savings on Housing-Related Expenses by:·······71

Chapter 6  Transportation ··············································74
           A. Transportation's Relevance to Savings Guide?·············75
           B. What Type of Vehicle Should You Purchase to
           Keep Costs in Check? ····································77
           C. The Importance of "Living Below" Your Transportation Means···78
           D. Opportunity Costs – Why They Matter ···················78
           E. "Investing the Difference" – A Smart Move for Extra Savings ·····79
           F. Used over New? – It's not that Simple ···················80
           G. Buy Versus Lease?······································81
           H. Negotiating Tips ·······································81
           I. Importance of Keeping Your Car in Excellent Condition ·········83
           J. Saving on Car Insurance ·································84
           K. Miscellaneous Transportation-Related Savings Tips: ·············84

Phase III   The Final Stages - Constructing a Quality Roof: (Full Maturation and Family Growth - Enjoying Life's Luxuries)· · · · · · · · · · · · · · · · · ·87

Chapter 7   Entertainment/Non-Essential Services · · · · · · · · · · · · · · · · · · · · ·89
     A. Doing Without - "Made Easy"· · · · · · · · · · · · · · · · · · · · · · · · · · · ·90
     B. Dining Out in Affordable Fashion · · · · · · · · · · · · · · · · · · · · · · ·91
     C. Vacationing for Less · · · · · · · · · · · · · · · · · · · · · · · · · · · · · · · · · ·92
     D. Staying Anchored By:· · · · · · · · · · · · · · · · · · · · · · · · · · · · · · · · ·93
     E. Successful "On Topic" Savings Techniques with Broad Applicability · · · · · · · · · · · · · · · · · · · · · · · · · · · · · · · · · · · · · ·94
     F. Miscellaneous Considerations: · · · · · · · · · · · · · · · · · · · · · · · · · · ·97

Chapter 8   Marriage/Friends· · · · · · · · · · · · · · · · · · · · · · · · · · · · · · · · · · · · · · ·100
     A. Financial Impact of Relationships – "For Better or For Worse"· · ·101
     B. Are You Commitment-Worthy? · · · · · · · · · · · · · · · · · · · · · · · · ·102
     C. The High Cost of Divorce · · · · · · · · · · · · · · · · · · · · · · · · · · · · ·103
     D. Commonality – The Relationship "Glue" · · · · · · · · · · · · · · · · · ·106
     E. Stress - The Best Compatibility Test · · · · · · · · · · · · · · · · · · · · · ·116
     F. Prenuptial Agreements – Do You Need One? · · · · · · · · · · · · · · · ·118
     G. Relationship "Saving" Pointers · · · · · · · · · · · · · · · · · · · · · · · · · ·121

Chapter 9   Children· · · · · · · · · · · · · · · · · · · · · · · · · · · · · · · · · · · · · · · · · · · · · ·124
     A. Overview · · · · · · · · · · · · · · · · · · · · · · · · · · · · · · · · · · · · · · · · · · ·125
     B. Avoid "Enabling" – In the Negative Sense of the Word · · · · · · · · ·126
     C. Their Failure is Your Failure? · · · · · · · · · · · · · · · · · · · · · · · · · · ·127
     D. Invest in Your Children's Success · · · · · · · · · · · · · · · · · · · · · · · ·128
     E. Saving without Sacrificing Quality or Safety · · · · · · · · · · · · · · · · ·131
     F. Important but Unrelated Thoughts · · · · · · · · · · · · · · · · · · · · · · ·133

     Summary · · · · · · · · · · · · · · · · · · · · · · · · · · · · · · · · · · · · · · · · · · · ·137
     Appendix A· · · · · · · · · · · · · · · · · · · · · · · · · · · · · · · · · · · · · · · · · · ·141
     Appendix B· · · · · · · · · · · · · · · · · · · · · · · · · · · · · · · · · · · · · · · · · · ·143
     About the Author· · · · · · · · · · · · · · · · · · · · · · · · · · · · · · · · · · · · ·145

# Acknowledgements

A special thanks to my amazingly supportive wife, Caroline, who made this work possible in more ways than one. Despite carrying a heavy load tending to a demanding full time job, she somehow found the time and energy on nights and weekends to provide our children with extra attention so I could focus on writing this book. Not an easy task considering our youngest was still an infant when this first took hold. And, words alone can't describe how appreciative and fortunate I am that Caroline also somehow managed to break free from her other obligations to serve as my trusted advisor/confidant, reviewing drafts and making meaningful recommendations for improvement. Additionally, a heartfelt thank you to my one-of-a-kind parents, Douglas and Joan Manning, who instilled a sense of financial responsibility in me (and so much more) since birth that has permeated my every fiber and to my in-laws, John and Joan Barna, for doing the same with my better half. Without my parents' unconditional love, tireless training and wealth of advice, I would not be where I am today. And this guide, just a fleeting thought … If at all. Lastly, I'm deeply indebted to my brother Scott Manning and friends Bill Motter, Pankaj Amin and Yvette Liebesman for providing invaluable advice along the way.

# Message to My Children

(Provides context for book)

*Dear Douglas and Tyler,*

*Although we share the same surname as Peyton and Eli, I was not raised by a father who could teach me how to throw a football like an NFL quarterback. My dad, your grandpa, was not an elite athlete, but he was a top performer in the workplace (more on that later). And, even if he could have somehow taught me the tricks of the trade like Archie, I would not have been able to do much with them in the long run given my physical stature.*

*Fortunately, Grandpa continually reinforced with me when I was young the importance of, among other things, being able to both earn and save a dollar. He grew up relatively poor by many standards and wanted to ensure that the cycle of financial struggles he personally witnessed his parents endure was broken for good in our family.*

*Did he accomplish this objective so I could continue in his footsteps of financial success? Absolutely, by leading by example and letting his actions, not mere words do the majority of the talking and influencing.*

*At one point in his career, Grandpa was one of the top sales performers in the nation in his industry/product line (sunscreen additives/pearlescent pigments) and his tireless work ethic was readily apparent to all who knew him. He would spend considerable time in his home office after hours speaking to clients, formulating sales strategies and otherwise honing his craft by staying abreast of the latest developments in the industry. As a result, I experienced the good fortune of being raised in an upper-middle class family.*

*However, Grandpa was careful not to soften me with excesses. I did not receive an allowance and was still expected to perform regular chores for the good of the family without compensation. Kids who are spoiled, he would say, are much more likely to fail later in life than those who are "hungry" and have to work for it. As a result, I was constantly exposed to invaluable learning experiences that helped shape me into who I* am today. These same experiences will also benefit you two boys for years to come as I pass them down the line in this Savings Guide or "Guide" for short.

Mom and I have been officially debt free since October 2008 at the ages of 41 and 35 respectively. (Could have been sooner if we did not make certain speculative investment decisions.) We own our home, cars and other possessions outright today and are not indebted to anyone, including credit card companies. Barring tragedy, we do not anticipate owing money to others ever again thanks to the lessons learned from our parents during our formative years.

After successfully applying and fine tuning those lessons for nearly two decades (and learning from our mistakes), the time has come to reduce them to writing to provide a consolidated blueprint for savings success to benefit you and your future families/children when we are long gone. Why the formality of penning this to paper? What gets written tends to be more clear and concise than verbal communications and is easier to study, revisit, share and measure progress against as you mature.

It is also our intention to share our message with other teenagers and young adults who may not be as fortunate as you. Some parents are unable to teach their children how to save money. They may be living pay check to pay check for a variety of reasons (poor health, did not apply themselves in school years earlier when it counted the most) or are simply too consumed with their jobs to make the time to do so. Giving is more gratifying than receiving and those who have done well (like your parents) have a moral obligation to assist those who have not and are willing to help themselves.

As you read this guide, please note it is designed as a beginning point for productive dialogue between you, me and Mom and was intentionally written at an adult level so you will further "grow" from the experience. Keep in mind there are no guarantees in life and it is perfectly acceptable and healthy to challenge the opinions of others, including your parents. All we ask is that you be open minded to receiving and acting upon our advice. There are countless examples of privileged children from well-off families that have not been able to replicate the earning and savings success of their parents.

Love you FOREVER,

Dad & Mom

P.S. **Saving is important, but money isn't everything. Put people first and enjoy life with them to its fullest!** On your death bed, you will summon loved ones, not cold, heartless stacks of cash.

# Preface

This book was originally written for the exclusive benefit of my two young sons (for their eyes only) to increase the likelihood they, too, will be able to live the great American Dream in a debt free manner. As fewer and fewer jobs pay a "living wage" and the basic costs of survival (food, shelter and transportation) continue to rise, this dream is becoming so very difficult to attain and hold on to with each passing year

The middle class is under attack and dwindling fast as the divide between rich and poor is growing at an alarming rate. To make matters worse - Healthcare and college tuition costs are increasing for most of us at a time we can least afford them. And, many, many parents are struggling to save for a "rainy day", while being stretched incredibly thin juggling family and career responsibilities in a rapidly changing work/technology environment. As a result, some parents (perhaps your very own) are over-relying on an already strained public education system to teach their children what they should be learning at home, like a deep rooted respect for the value of a dollar and sound money management principles.

How can you ensure you don't get left behind financially in this day and age of economic uncertainty? For starters - By adhering to a proven "savings plan" that is 50 plus years in the making. A plan that is holistic and comprehensive in nature and focuses on building lasting wealth from the ground up at an early age … Starting with a solid personal foundation, sturdy frame and quality roof so you are someday sheltered from destructive storms and other damaging elements, whether naturally occurring or man-made.

The good news: No matter how dire things become economically here in the United States and beyond, there will always be newcomers that successfully battle the odds and rise to the top financially. I sacrificed countless nights and weekends over the course of three busy years writing this guide (while somehow managing my full time day job, aiding my mother in her losing battle with cancer and assisting in introducing my second son to the world), because I strongly believe it will significantly improve the odds my children will be able to save enough money at an early enough age to enjoy the liberating experience of financial independence/freedom (synonymous with living debt free) … just like I have and my parents before me.

As a way of giving back to others, I'm sharing my message with you so you too can stack the cards in your favor so you can enjoy a brighter future … A future where you are not living paycheck to paycheck or worrying about where your next meal is coming from. A future where you are proud to be classified as middle class or better and are able to fend for yourself upon completing your formal schooling. A future filled with sound financial and lifestyle decisions that will positively impact you and your future loved ones for years to come!

Still not convinced and wondering why you should listen to my advice? Plain and simple, it works. (I wouldn't subject my kids to it otherwise.) My Dad successfully piloted this thought provoking savings plan with me growing up and I have been able to replicate/refine to a large degree. Why re-invent the wheel when it has proven to be tremendously beneficial through two generations? You need a proven system *now*, not later. You don't have as much time as you think to tinker with various strategies. It's harder to change or adjust your ways the older you get. And besides - Is doing nothing (maintaining the status quo) a viable option? Will quick fixes or oversimplified, one dimensional approaches put you at increased risk of doing worse than your parents or becoming enslaved or indebted to others for most or all of your life?

If you are truthful with yourself, you are probably aware you tend to discount your parent's advice, no matter how logical or sound. Hearing some of it again, from a neutral third party like me, may encourage you to listen and follow it all the more. Nothing I'm sharing is new or novel. However, surely some of it is what your well-off neighbors might not feel comfortable telling you or your family. If I wasn't in the know as a teenager or young adult, I would want to read this book as soon as possible to get off to a fast start in life.

# Introduction

One of the hardest parts of becoming financially independent (zero debt) is saving money. The hardest part of saving money is knowing how to do so and successfully executing upon that knowledge. (No different than following a diet to lose weight.)

To successfully execute a sound savings plan (the major point of failure for most), *you* must be patient, focused and disciplined and adhere to a mindset that rejects materialism. And, you must start studying and applying some of the savings principles in this guide while you are young (ideally in junior high school), so they stick with you for a lifetime and yield big pay-offs in adulthood.

You can't save decent money unless you make decent money. And, you will have difficulty making decent money unless you do the right things while you are living at home under your parents' care. If you have not established a solid academic record, begun preparing for your career and developed healthy habits *before* life after high school, college or trade school - It will be much harder to get back on track later on. Especially as America's middle-class is rapidly dwindling, companies are reducing employee benefits and being able to retire comfortably at a reasonable age like your grandparents is becoming a thing of the past.

Although you will no doubt have to work very hard to enjoy the same high standard of living as previous generations, you can continue to experience a quality life through the power of saving and being thrifty. No one knows what the future holds. Even the experts can't predict with any degree of accuracy what lies ahead. Don't worry about what you can't control. Focus on excelling in areas you can control - namely your own financial destiny.

Everyone wants to make more money, but very few are willing to work for it. Doing so requires making difficult personal sacrifices while focusing on elevating your earning power to the next level. If you act like everyone else and take the easy route, you will earn an average wage and be unable to save to the extent necessary to attain Early Financial Independence (EFI).

## What this saving guide IS:

- **A review of the top nine focus areas to becoming a successful saver:** Education/Career, Health (Mental and Physical), Investment Vehicles, Food/Essentials, Housing/Shelter, Transportation/Mobility, Entertainment/Services, Marriage/Friends and Children. They are listed in order of relative "purchase" importance and or consideration significance to someone attending junior high or high-school, the ideal time to read this guide. The first three key areas are all about investing in yourself while your parents are taking care of your basic needs. The middle three are more of a concern when you are living on your own after high-school or college. The final three are most applicable when you have become somewhat established in your career and have started your own family.
- **A "case study" in analyzing consumption decisions related to the aforementioned nine areas.** Although certain principles or techniques may become outdated over time, the logic and reasoning presented herein can be applied to new circumstances. The ability to think on your feet and question things that don't seem to make sense, for instance, will not only improve your critical thinking skills and lead to increased confidence – but also preserve your hard earned capital and make it work for you when you need it most.
- **A lesson in the importance of not getting caught up in our current culture of materialism and sticking to the basics, such as establishing purchasing priorities and learning to live below your means.** If you can't afford a non-essential, don't buy it! Spending in today's society is all too often inaccurately equated with happiness and success. Produce your own happiness through accomplishments, not acquiring things. Too many people spend first, and then attempt to save for it when the reverse should be taking place. Debt enslaves us and extra possessions weigh us down.
- **A means of supplementing your K through 12 education.** Public and private schools are primarily focused on preparing you for college or vocational school, not teaching holistic, broad based money management skills that include sound savings principles. Their carefully crafted curriculums are designed to teach you the basics/fundamentals so one day you can apply them to a career and become a productive member of society. This guide teaches

you "how to fish" concerning personal finances and related Life 101 decisions so you never go hungry.

## What this saving guide is NOT:

- **How to become rich by learning the next great investment strategy.** If you want to become a multi-millionaire, you can take several paths. Becoming an indispensable superstar in your profession, working on Wall Street, taking on tremendous risk (entrepreneurial), marrying up or doing something highly illegal (Bernie Madoff's Pyramid scheme) are always options. But when it comes to striking true investment riches, either luck or insider trading usually play a big role and the major downside to failing to hit it big is you are more apt to lose everything in the process ... including your freedom. If Investment Gurus can't guarantee their own financial success – What makes you think you can?
- **An easy "x" step plan to financial freedom.** Nothing worth obtaining is ever easy and there are no guarantees in life, except your eventual death. Step plans help sell books since people prefer clarity (black and white) to ambiguity (grey) and are constantly searching for secret "ingredients" when none exist. If only obtaining Early Financial Independence (EFI) were as simple as following a tried and true recipe ... like the one for Toll House chocolate chip cookies.
- **A blueprint for achieving overall "success" in life.** There are many different ways to define success and attaining EFI is not in and of itself an indication of such. How empty would life be if your bank accounts were one day overflowing, but you neglected to establish meaningful relationships with friends and family along the way? I once spoke to a high profile Lawyer who routinely worked 100 hour weeks for years on end to the disappointment of his children, who eventually severed ties with him as adults. Even though he gave them plenty of money, they could not overlook the lack of time he spent with them when they were young, impressionable and vulnerable. Their rationale – "You were not there for us Dad when we needed you the most, why should we be there for you now that the tables are turned? As his career was winding down, he was hoping to make amends by bonding with his grandchildren ... a bond that might never be because of misplaced priorities years earlier with his own children.
- **How to retire early and live comfortably ever after.** Retiring early can be a risky proposition. There are too many variables and assumptions to account for over long stretches of time where change is the only constant. If you retire at age 55, for instance, but live to 85 – You will have likely spent the same amount of time working as fading off into the sunset. What happens if you

run out of money at the age of 75 and are unable to earn additional income by re-entering the workforce? Try to select a profession that you really like, pays well and values the wisdom associated with aging gracefully (i.e., Law, Engineering, scientific research, skilled trades) because you may be at it longer than you think. Those that believe they can hit it big and walk away early from the "daily grind" are in for a big disappointment. Plan for the worst and select a career that you can be engaged in until you are at least 62.

- **An inspirational set of beliefs for attaining true happiness.** Like success, happiness can prove to be elusive. Money and material goods in and of themselves can't ensure happiness, although they can provide you with more satisfying life experiences, like partaking in enriching travel destinations, relaxing massages and adventurous dining out experiences (all non-possessions.) Happiness is a state of mind. The more positive your thoughts, especially around the area of appreciating what you have (and not fixating on what you don't have), the better off you'll be.
- **About how to maximize your rate of personal savings.** The word maximize suggests doing *everything* in your power to reduce expenses and save money even if it means doing without what most people would consider modern necessities. If your *only* goal in life were to accumulate as much money as possible without spending and enjoying it, would life be worth living? There is no reward for those who die with the biggest bank account or most toys. Seize the day and *optimize* ("as effective or practical as possible") your savings rate by making rational decisions that take into consideration goals other than socking away as much money as possible.

In closing, becoming financially independent at an early age (and remaining so) is an amazingly worthwhile goal that is well within your reach if you: 1) Are motivated enough to reap the benefits associated with it. 2) Truly believe that "stuff" does not equal wealth and happiness. 3) And, are disciplined and open minded enough *to follow* practical advice.

The world is full of people with big dreams who can't muster up enough courage to take even one positive step in the right direction to fulfill them. Whether their collective inaction is due to being risk averse, unorganized or just plain lazy really doesn't matter. INACTION USUALLY ALWAYS RESULTS IN FAILURE. The choice is yours. You can follow the advice in this savings guide and very likely never have to worry about money again or do nothing. Which one is it going to be?

# Phase I

The Early Stages, Laying a Solid Foundation:

(Your Teenage Years & Beyond – Working on the Basics)

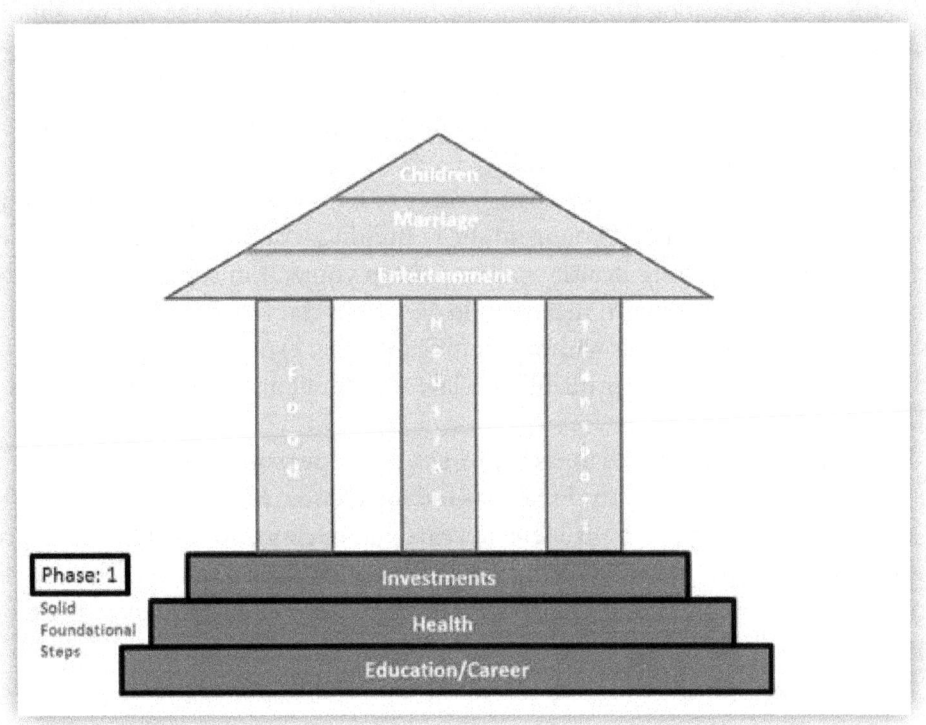

Building & maintaining EFI by managing your "spend"/focus on your personal foundation.

You can't build a stable home without first laying a solid foundation for everything else to rest on for support. The foundation absorbs the full weight of the structure and all occupants and possessions benefit immensely from its proper installation and the fundamental stability it provides. If a contractor cuts too many corners on the foundation, the defects may be impossible to correct later without razing the entire structure.

The same holds true for your savings success. If you don't spend enough time in school as you transition into a young adult: 1) Building your academic brand when it counts most, 2) Developing healthy habits to keep yourself in top mental and physical strength and 3) Learning to make sound *basic* financial investments - you may not be able to reverse course later without significant time, expense and pain. When you reach your 30's and 40's, it is probably too late to rebuild and achieve the goal of this guide.

The aforementioned three areas represent your **"personal foundation"** for savings success and resulting Early Financial Independence. If you succeed in learning and applying these basics in your teenage years and beyond, you will be one-third of the way down the path to experiencing a wonderful debt free existence. You can do it! "A journey of a thousand miles begins with a single step" (Laozi) Take your first one today and you will never regret it.

# CHAPTER 1

## Education/Career

*When it comes to doing well in this category, developing a solid study/work ethic is of utmost importance. There are no "free lunches" in the ultra-competitive world of academia and business.*

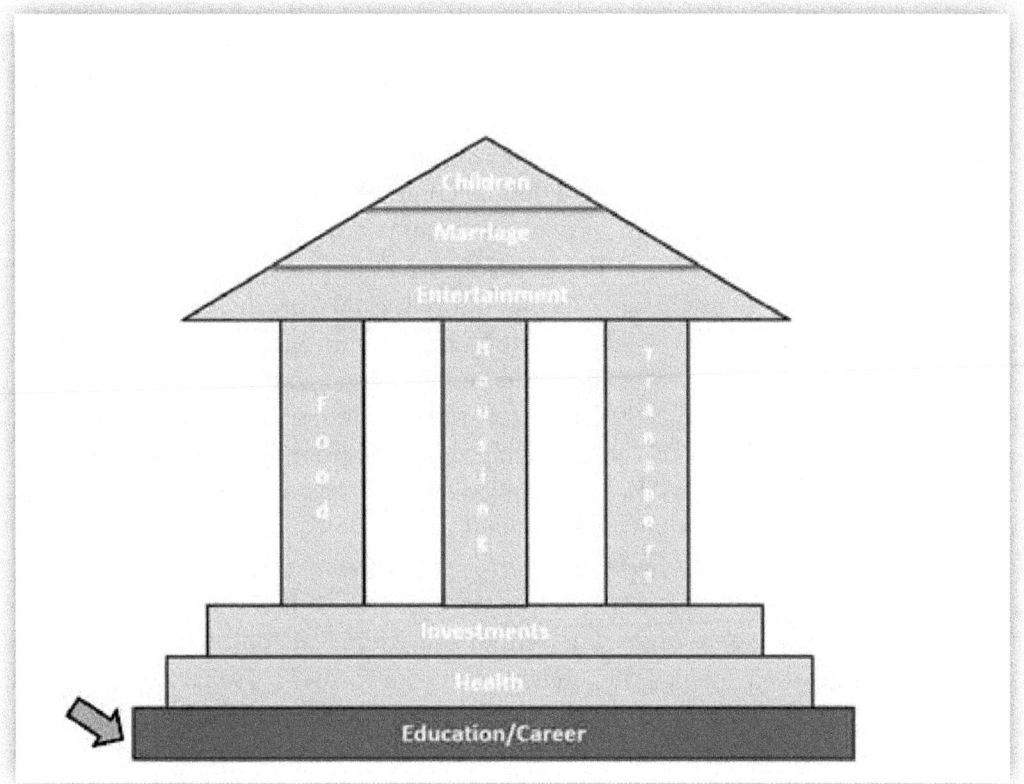

Building & maintaining EFI by managing your "spend"/focus on your education/career.

## A. Up to Secondary School (Through High School)

What do education and career have to do with savings success? More than you could possibly imagine at this stage of your life. Quite simply, you can't save money if you don't have a good job. And, you typically can't get a good job unless you have a solid education/training in a profession or skilled trade that is in demand.

If you were to enter the workforce today with only your high school diploma in hand, your career options would be limited and your earnings potential, low. A very large pool of candidates (anyone with a basic high school degree) would be competing with you to fill the same low skilled positions, like waiter/waitress, gas station attendant, or retail store associate. Most US citizens have a high school diploma, because it is compulsory and free. Fewer have a college degree and beyond (i.e., MBA, JD or MD) due to the added cost, effort and sacrifice required to obtain one.

Set yourself apart from the pack! The minimum cost of renting a small one bedroom starter apartment in a safe neighborhood, for instance, may be 12K per year by the time you need one (picking an arbitrary number to make a point) and does *not* factor into consideration your individual level of education and career choice. If you become a sales associate at a retail clothing store earning 15-20K per year, you will not be able to live on your own and save money unless you share an apartment and utilities with a roommate. Even then, your costs may exceed your income, resulting in the early accumulation of additional debt beyond school loans.

If on the other end of the educational spectrum you were to obtain a highly marketable degree, such as Chemical Engineering, your starting annual salary *might* be 80-90K by the time you graduate ... as that figure was 60-70K in 2012. There would be fewer folks in society who would be able to measure up against you educationally, so your long term earning prospects would be quite good, and you would be able to start saving money right away. 90K may seem like a lot, but after deducting federal and state taxes, in addition to routine living expenses (rent, utilities, food, car and insurance) **and school loans** - You may only be able to save 5% to 10% of what you make! (Still, much better than not saving at all.)

The moral of the story - *Spend your early years positioning yourself educationally for a lucrative career when all you have to worry about is yourself.* When you are married and have kids, it's not so easy to go back to school and pursue an additional degree. Your priorities change when you have dependents and your former personal time becomes, for the most part, their time ... That is if you want to keep your family together.

If you must go back to school and re-tool with a young family in tow, it is not impossible. Just be prepared for your newfound personal study sacrifice to become their sacrifice as well and result in extra tension around the house as your spouse takes on additional responsibilities, much like a single parent. Anything worth obtaining comes with a cost. However, proceed with caution when others are impacted by your decisions!

On a positive note, you should have plenty of time in high school and your freshman year of college to align yourself with a major that plays to your strengths *and* leads to meaningful employment. In the meantime, why not use your junior high school years to learn as much as you can and identify subjects you excel in? In my personal experience (as I look back on my academic performance and those of my classmates), there is a positive correlation between getting good grades in junior high and doing the same in high school, a springboard for getting admitted into an excellent college.

Good habits (i.e., solid study routines), like bad habits, tend to stick with you for a long time. And since both take a fair degree of effort to undo, it pays to get it right the first time around. It's difficult catching-up academically once you have fallen behind. A poor junior high school student generally makes for a poor high school student and the same holds true further up the educational chain. A poor high school student most likely can't turn it around in college and may have a hard time obtaining meaningful employment upon graduation unless a skilled trade route is pursued. (More on skilled trades later.)

You will have plenty of time to explore the world after you complete your formal education. It may not seem that way now, since school is all you know and emancipation feels like a universe away. But rest assured, you will be able to shift priorities to other pursuits someday, and that day is coming sooner than you think. Until then, enjoy your teenage years, focus on **investing in yourself** academically and avoid the many temptations along the way to derail the temporary "free ride" (or partial subsidy) funded by your parents. Although you need to be patient (a virtue worth developing), since doing well in school or a particular subject may not come easy or happen overnight - The end result can last a lifetime and is worth the effort.

## B. Post-Secondary School (College & Graduate Studies)

Gone are the days simply attending *a* college was enough to set you apart from the crowd, ensuring you'll do well. Many high school seniors skipped college in the 1940's through 1970's (and to some extent the 80's) and directly entered the workforce into well-paying manufacturing jobs and related "blue-collar" occupations. This made the prospect of foregoing a steady income for 2-4 years, while pursuing an "extra" diploma, seem like too high a sacrifice to some.

Almost everything today, however, is made abroad in countries like China, Japan, and Germany. Therefore, it should come as no surprise there are correspondingly far fewer manufacturing jobs available now in the United States and as a result - More students are staying in school longer. When these students graduate with either an undergraduate or graduate degree, they are chasing a limited number of entry-level service and/or professional opportunities, which are also ironically being outsourced/smart shored abroad at an increasing rate.

The end result - College is now the new high school. Consequently, be ultra-selective where you apply and what you major in. Not all educational experiences are created equal and will lead to Early Financial Independence. Too many students go to college because, it is the next step after high school, everyone else is doing it and the experience will supposedly help them find themselves. Besides, what has worked well in the past, some surmise, must surely work now and in the future from a career and income earning advantage standpoint. (Since when is it a smart move to follow the masses without questioning whether or not it is the best course of action or inaction for you?)

Attending college can be a very enriching experience when done right! It builds confidence, teaches you how to think logically and sharpens interpersonal skills. Most importantly, if you select a course of study that is in demand and has a solid "return on investment" (ROI), it can open many doors for you upon graduation and lead to a well-paying entry level job. *The latter of which should be your number one reason for attending college.* In other words, pursue a major highly coveted by potential employers so you can land a good paying job, begin re-paying your college loans in short order and realize a positive return on your educational spend. (Pick a course of study you also like that develops critical thinking skills as you will be doing it for a long time … Income earning prospects should not be the only factor in making this decision.)

Your selection of a major is one of the most important decisions you will ever make, right behind your career track and choice of life partner. When you are married with children, there is little time (and often money) to reposition yourself by going back to school and pursuing another major. It's hard enough changing careers that leverage the same major for reasons beyond the scope of this guide. So, make the very most of your initial selection and don't assume you will be able to attend graduate school (any advanced education beyond college).

Some students pick an easy collegiate major with an eye towards "artificially" boosting their grade point average so their transcript looks more attractive to graduate schools. Are high grades your primary objective? What if you graduate college with a perfect 4.0 in an easy major that is not very marketable (translation: low paying work) AND you can't pay back your school loans due to poor job prospects? What have you accomplished? Taking the easy route with your undergraduate major is a risky move that can negatively impact your future earnings power and savings rate.

College is not cheap. It is highly likely the total cost of obtaining a four year degree (tuition, room & board, books, lost income and interest on loans) will be the second most costly purchase you ever make, right behind a home/residence. Therefore, spend adequate time while you can (preferably while still in high school) researching "profitable" majors that you are a good fit for.

Traditionally, Science and Math graduates have been in high demand, because so few students pursue these disciplines. As a result, technical degrees in Biology and Engineering, have historically out-earned Liberal Arts degrees, such as English and History ... and I suspect (no proof/statistics) even when the latter are obtained from upper echelon Ivy League schools. However, labor shortages existing in the United States today are being filled by large multi-national corporations with students in as far-away places as India and China, who value a technical education. So stay informed. What is in demand today in our global economy may not be in demand when you are ready to attend college. And, **if you don't adapt to changing circumstances and stay ahead of the curve, you will be left behind no matter how talented or intellectually gifted you are**.

During the Great depression, farming was the number one occupation in the United States. Due to rapid advances in farm technology (bigger tractors, chemical pesticides and man-made fertilizers) and the emergence of large corporate-backed farms, millions of "mom and pop" farmers have been put out of business since then. It was not because they did not know their trade well enough or were unwilling to work longer, harder hours to stay afloat - External game changing influences essentially made most individual small farms obsolete. If you decided to pursue a course of study in farming, where would you be down the road knowing that less than 1% of all Americans make a living off the land today?

The same can be said for millions of Liberal Arts college students, who graduate with degrees each year in Art History, Western Literature, English or Dance hoping that "if they build it" (obtain a degree in the aforementioned majors), "they will come" (employers will offer jobs). Real life does not often mirror the movies (Field of Dreams, in this case) where Hollywood has the ability to craft happy endings at will. The fact is: there is a lessening of demand for certain degrees no matter how well they train you to think on your feet *or* where you obtain them from.

I'm not suggesting the type of college you attend is unimportant. A two year associate degree from a community college does not carry as much weight as a four year degree from a top tier institution for obvious reasons. However, being one of the best in your field of studies at a top college does not ensure a high paying job will await you if there are extremely limited job openings for it in the first place. You can't control supply and demand when it comes to majors and occupations.

There are plenty of Ivy League graduates with an English degree vying for the very same associate professor openings ... usually after paying for a Masters/PhD program, a significant additional cost/investment. Do your homework before selecting a major. This will increase the chances your hard work and sacrifice pay off in the end. Don't select today's occupational equivalent of "farmer", even if it plays to your passions and strengths.

"Do what you love and money will follow" is often flawed advice. If you love acting, for instance, and spend your most productive years studying the craft and pursuing movie roles - What happens if you don't succeed in the end? What is the opportunity cost (lost income) associated with pursuing such a path? Hopefully somewhat manageable if you invested along the way in a backup plan (a necessity no matter what your focus is) and are willing to play catch-up. You are more likely to get *lucky* selecting a winning pick six lottery ticket than landing a high paying acting role in a Hollywood movie or TV series.

The expression "Do what you love ..." in this context should be modified to **"Select a course of study you excel at, are passionate about *and* is likely to lead to a high paying job"** either upon graduation or a few years down the road based on labor supply and market demand forecasts. (I.e., as measured by a large volume of anticipated job openings versus a relatively small number of projected qualified applicants.) If you truly excel at something and are paid well (a form of recognition or validation), the love will follow! To summarize: Selecting a financially viable and sustainable career path that plays to your unique strengths is the name of the game! You shouldn't "mortgage" your future by attending college hoping to find yourself and the right major. Hope is not a successful strategy.

If by your junior or senior year of high school you are struggling academically, still searching for your strengths or are unsure of your major/course of study in college, consider enrolling in a local community college for a year or two. You may need extra time to blossom/mature and uncover what you do best before transferring to a more challenging four year university. Conversely, you may decide this collegiate "dry run" of sorts taught you an invaluable lesson - A traditional 4 year degree is not for you and you have other talents worth exploring.

There is nothing wrong with enrolling in a trade school or Vo-tech program offered through your high school. Not everyone is academically gifted. Electricians, plumbers and carpenters, for example, are highly sought after and make high hourly wages (not bound by geography) that can support you and your future family. The majority of the US-born population has bought into the notion that a college education is necessary to be successful (even if that is not their strength) and have moved away from pursuing the skilled trades. This leads to a smaller supply of trained tradespeople in occupations that cannot be outsourced abroad very easily

To be successful as an independent tradesman you need to be highly dependable and possess solid interpersonal skills to sell your service. If you can help it, don't work long term for someone else beyond your apprentice period. The real money is in running your own business and building your own reliable, trusted brand. Therefore, if you decide to pursue a skilled trade and you want the independence of being your own boss, also carve out time (perhaps at night) to take business and accounting classes so you are in the best possible position to be your own boss someday if that interests you.

## C. Important Career Factors - Industry, On-Going Training & Balance

Obviously, being employed in higher paying careers/occupations/professions ("jobs", hereafter) enables you to save more money, and at a faster rate, than lower paying jobs. What many people fail to recognize, however, until they are much further along in their careers - The pay provided for essentially performing the same job function varies significantly by industry.

**Importance of working for high profit margin industries** - Not all industries are equally as profitable. Some are "squeezed" by perennially high operating costs and increased competition, while others enjoy more favorable market conditions brought on by increased regulation and significant start-up barriers. A client-facing consumer retail sales position, for instance, pays far less on average than a sales position in the pharmaceutical industry. There is partially attributed to the fact that there is less of a markup on flat screen TVs (a commodity that can be purchased elsewhere), than patent-protected prescription drugs that are unique in their efficacy and can only be acquired from one source (a temporary legal monopoly designed to spur innovation). It also requires more skill and specialized knowledge to convince doctors and or medical establishments to prescribe certain drugs over others, hence the additional pay difference.

In short, follow the money! Profit margins (the percentage a product or service is marked up beyond cost) dictate how handsomely an employer can afford to reward you from a total compensation standpoint. The higher the average profit margin in an industry, the more lucrative it will be for you to work in that space. And, base pay is only one component of compensation that facilitates greater savings. Higher profit margin industries also tend to offer better perks. They do this in the form of providing employees with more attractive commission, profit sharing and stock option offerings as well as more valuable traditional benefit plans. An employer's contributions to your healthcare, retirement and leave entitlement plans (VAC, Sick, STD, etc.), although somewhat "hidden", can be quite sizable over time saving you big dollars in the process.

If you are going to work hard in your job - Why not pick an industry that can afford to pay you more for the same responsibilities? It's not all about what you do and how hard you work at perfecting your trade. Often times the *where* you do it is as important as anything else.

**Importance of continuing education and "viability" monitoring** - Once you land the right job in the right industry, continue to invest in yourself by enrolling in on-going training programs *and* actively monitoring the job/industry for future viability. Learning should not stop after college, particularly in relation to your career. If you don't make it a regular life-long pursuit, you risk stagnating (no promotions) and jeopardizing your future earnings stream and savings power by becoming less relevant and employable in your field. The business world, and the technologies that support it, are changing at a rapid pace. Failure to keep up with the skill sets of newer workforce entrants and savvy re-tooled veterans will make you less marketable and quite possibly, obsolete/unemployable.

How many computer programmers solely schooled in FORTRAN or COBOL mainframe technology (popular in the 1980's) are employed today? Surely far fewer than the number of IT professionals who started out in their shoes, but learned along the way to become proficient in more modern, in demand client/server languages, such as Java or Visual Basic. The same could be said of today's programmers who fail to keep up with tomorrow's promising technologies, no matter what names are eventually used to describe them.

Most major corporations encourage their employees to participate in on-going training and continuous self- improvement programs. Talent Management initiatives are the strategic norm and formalized Learning and Performance programs (some compulsory) are often in place for you to take advantage of. However, don't stop there! Corporate sponsored training only runs so deep in a particular subject matter due to ever present time and financial constraints.

Therefore, avail yourself of the extensive resources and specialized subject matter experts routinely provided by relevant professional associations and traditional educational institutions. Employers often subsidize these efforts through tuition reimbursement programs if you maintain a certain grade point average. Obtaining a graduate degree or certification in your field distinguishes you from your peers and tends to signify you possess additional insight regarding industry best practices and trends. In turn, this makes you more valuable to your employer and their clients and is often rewarded by a pay increase.

**Importance of learning basic sales skills -** One training subject you should definitely pursue regardless of your line of work and job title is the fundamentals of selling (also referred to as "Sales 101" techniques). Even if you do not work in a sales or sales related capacity, if you can effectively persuade individuals or organizations to buy a service, product or idea from you (preferably in a face-to-face setting) - You can parlay this talent into success in other important areas. *All jobs require some degree of sales acumen to excel at them.*

Although as an Engineer, for instance, you may not interface with external clients, you will surely have to satisfy internal clients, like your boss, fellow associates (from both within and outside your own department) and third party partners. Their ability to complete an important task/milestone may be contingent upon your ability as Team Lead to articulate the proposed benefits of an action or inaction in a persuasive and likeable manner. If you can't do so, the project may stall or fail, hampering your career in the process. Companies with a strong service culture recognize the importance of treating internal clients with the same kid gloves as external clients. The sooner you master this, the better off you'll be.

It takes years to become a solid salesperson. Why not start practicing some of the techniques when you are in high school? The ability to succinctly convey the feature/benefits of what you are selling, handling objections in an acceptable manner and building up enough confidence to ask for an "order" ... often from complete strangers ... comes with time. And as you will find, success begets success as your positive energies carry over from one sale to the next. You can start selling by volunteering to raise funds for an extra-curricular activity (I.e., Little League booster stickers, school newspaper subscriptions, American Cancer Society walk-a-thon, etc.) by going door to door and soliciting donations or sponsorships from neighbors.

Now back to the central theme of this chapter, optimizing savings through smart education and career track decisions. Hopefully you are convinced selecting the right major/trade leads to the right job. And targeted on-going training/learning (including Sales 101 skills) helps you hold onto that job by enhancing your overall performance and value to the team.

**Importance of excelling in your current job/role** - Furthermore, the best way to increase your savings is to earn more on the job income! (You can only get by on a fixed salary for so long before inflation starts eating you alive.) If after investing in yourself and your skill set you receive a larger than average annual merit increase from your boss, the payback can be substantial. Even at an entry level salary of say 40K, the difference between a 2% and 4% raise is $800. Sure it will be taxed and you may only take home an extra $450. But, think about how this extra amount will be compounded over time and equate to more in your next raise. And, more importantly, you will be one step closer to receiving a bigger payout some day in the form of a promotion. Repeated, consistent performance level increases, including accomplishments such as nailing "stretch assignments", stand out on your annual review and are visible to the entire organization, including other hiring managers.

**Work/life balance, a definite consideration over the long run** - Money is important, but not THE most important thing in life. You can't buy good health, quality relationships or more time in a day. However, money can *improve* health, *enhance* relationships and create *additional* leisure time, but only if your job is somewhat balanced over the long haul. If it is not, your health, happiness and relationships will surely suffer. Therefore, don't select a job/career path purely based on high income levels.

If as a corporate tax attorney, for example (not endorsing the profession or suggesting you become one), you are expected to bill 2500 hours per year (This is more than 48 hours per week, not including administrative time!) to attain partnership status in your firm, you may have to work most nights and weekends. This may be acceptable in your younger years when you don't have a family to support. But how about in your middle years when the title of Senior Partner regularly pulls you away from loved ones? And family aside, you must also ask - Is the added cost/burden associated with forgoing hobbies, social activities and normal routines (infrequent exercise and skipped meals) worth the additional income? In the short run, the answer is almost always "Yes". You must pay your dues and what better time to do so then when you are first starting out. It is much easier to let up on the gas some after you have tasted success (built up a good lead/savings cushion) than to go full throttle after years of "coasting" or moderation and trying to play catch-up.

A well-balanced work environment to consider transitioning to in middle age is the public sector. Federal, state and local jobs tend to offer more time off and other perks than their equivalent counterparts in the private sector. Less pay may be one of the tradeoffs, but richer back-end benefits (health insurance and guaranteed pensions) more than make up for it as of this writing. A corporate tax attorney, partner or no partner, can flip sides and work for the IRS or SEC. If they don't like the experience, they can always return to the private sector with additional insight and newfound connections.

Although there is nothing wrong with joining the public sector employment ranks immediately upon graduation from college (so you can retire early and perhaps collect a second pension in another role before you finally hang up your hat), don't discount the private sector. There are no guarantees in life and public sector benefits might become significantly diluted in the future without grandfather clauses. With the exception of the Federal government, State and Local entities may end up being forced to declare bankruptcy, thereby reneging on their pension promises and no-cost or low cost healthcare plan subsidies. The public sector can't continue down the same path without major changes. Therefore, if the private sector offers more lucrative salaries when you graduate, go for it!

Additionally, don't underestimate the desirability of parlaying your specialized talents into the teaching profession. A well respected private sector attorney can become a Law School Professor, or even a judge for that matter. (Not easy, but possible.) Although Professors have varying degrees of pressure early on in their career to become published and make a name for themselves, the paid time-off they are awarded in return, including "winter" breaks and periodic sabbaticals are without equal. And besides, after "x" years a professor may become tenured (property right in your job that varies by institution) which equates to additional job security when you may need it most … meaning as you age.

## D. Miscellaneous Considerations for Full Time Students
Other ways, by no means all inclusive, to get the biggest bang from your educational investment:

- **Emphasize success in the classroom over excelling in sports.** Although it is possible to do both if you are gifted, too many students spend a disproportionate amount of time improving their athletic skills at the expense of their grades. You have a better chance at winning the lottery than earning a decent living playing for a professional sports team. Coaching, recruiting and teaching (I.e., Physical Education) are among your best bets. However, if you excel at a sport, you might obtain a full or partial athletic scholarship, which can be worth a lot of money. But make sure it is not conditional on you making the team or staying healthy unless it can get you into a school/program that you ordinarily would not qualify for.
- **Apply for local scholarships and cast a wide net.** You never know who will ultimately recognize your accomplishments, if you treat this endeavor like a part time job.
- **While attending college, apply for a part time job on campus.** Aside from earning some well-needed spending money along the way, the job will enhance your first resume (increasing the likelihood of obtaining meaningful employment upon graduation).
- **Participate in cooperative education or internship programs.** You must differentiate yourself from the competition even while attending school so that your employment prospects are improved. You are no longer competing with students solely from the United States for work. In many cases, you are competing with the entire world. The Internet and cheap high speed bandwidth is a great equalizer that levels the playing field for all job seekers, including skilled professionals, from Doctors (radiologists read X-Rays from abroad) to remote software implementation specialists accessing servers many oceans away.
- **When considering graduate school, you are better served getting a job first.** This improves the odds of 1) Getting into a quality program and 2) Having your employer pay to send you back to school. Some companies offer significant monetary assistance from 50-100% tuition reimbursement. They may also grant you a sabbatical to attend school full time and even encourage you to pursue a professional degree (MBA, JD, PHD) to grow loyal talent from within to fill critical shortages.

The decision to pursue a particular path of post-secondary education should be all about analyzing whether it is prudent to spend a lot of borrowed money on yourself now to make even more in the future. If you don't believe the route/major you have chosen will enable such, choose a different route. Why spend $200,000 plus on a four year college degree ($50k per year, not including interest rate costs), plus an additional $80,000 in lost income (assuming minimum 20K starting annual salary right out of high school) when your short and long term job prospects are bleak? You know how long it takes to re-coup/payback $300,000? For some: An entire lifetime. The typical homeowner takes 30 or more years on average to pay off their house when this sum of money is borrowed. Final comment on the subject of Jobs - Academic success alone does not automatically correlate to real world business success. They are two separate animals. The latter has politics written all over it. Learn to play the game of successfully interacting with others in a high stakes professional environment.

# CHAPTER 2

# Health (Mental & Physical)

*One of the quickest ways to personal bankruptcy is through high health bills, even among the insured. Take good care of your body and it will return the favor.*

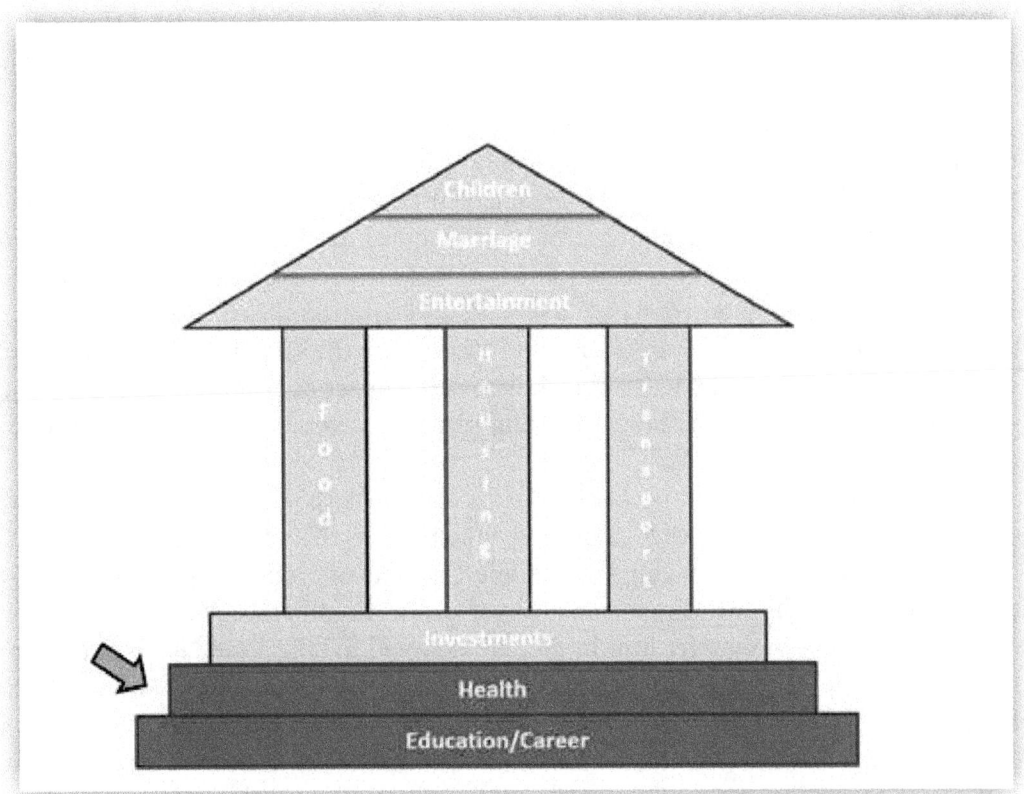

Building & maintaining EFI by managing your "spend"/focus on your health.

What does health have to do with your ability to save? Your body is the most important income generating asset you will ever possess. With a bit of luck and proper nurturing and maintenance, your mental and physical attributes will take you to great heights. When you are feeling well, you are able to study effectively, perform job functions at a high level and save a decent portion of your income. When you are not feeling well, studying and working is a challenge (if they can be performed at all), interfering with your income stream and ability to save, as excess money gets diverted to healthcare costs.

It pays to take good care of your body *and* interconnected emotional state/mind. Although you probably consider yourself invincible and take for granted the good health you have hopefully enjoyed thus far, things can change with the blink of an eye. One indiscretion, such as drinking and driving, can alter your life considerably and modern medicine (high tech drugs and specialized surgery) can only go so far in repairing damaged parts, especially the brain. Think before you act and do everything possible to protect your most precious investment – You! When you are "damaged", you can't trade yourself in for another "you" like you can with a car, appliance or electronic gadget.

In keeping with the theme of this guide, think of yourself as a precision all-in-one tool for building your own "home". If you are un-calibrated, blunt or broken due to an extended physical or mental illness, it will be much harder, if not impossible to construct what you need and control your financial destiny. If your "chainsaw" is missing a chain and you need to clear the lot of trees to prepare the foundation area - You might need to rely on your "ax", a less desirable option. It will surely take more time and effort (perhaps 100 times more) to accomplish the same result with even the sharpest of blades. And, if your "ax" is dull due to neglect or plain old forgetfulness, you may have to abort your home building plans all together. Have you ever tried chopping wood with a dull ax?

How do you ensure your proverbial "ax" is always sharp? Good health starts with eating the right foods and encompasses so much more than being physically fit. It includes to a larger extent, having a sound mind capable of producing consistent positive thoughts that honor the importance of perseverance and possessing a stellar work ethic. (Lazy people, no matter how bright, are doomed to fail.) There is a connection between lifestyle and health, and unfortunately this awareness is often lost in today's fast paced world.

When you don't eat right, exercise or get enough downtime to re-charge your batteries – Stress can get the better of you. Some stress is good, motivating you to perform at peak levels. Too much stress, however, has been linked to ailments such as: Heart disease, gastrointestinal disorders, depression, migraines, and more frequent colds - to name a few.

Why should we care about these ailments when there are medicines to treat them? Medicines don't treat the root cause of the problem, only the symptoms. And, there are side effects to using them, some of which can be dangerous. Additionally, medicine may not return you to a 100% healthy state and can't recoup lost time and productivity – The latter of which definitely impacts the quality of your performance in school and on the job. Think back to the last time you caught a cold and felt lethargic. Wasn't it more difficult to focus on your studies with a sore throat, cough and or congestion related "cobwebs" in your head? Could you imagine having to deal with similar symptoms every day of your life, despite being on meds, because you neglect your mind and body?

Minimize the possibility of poor health by focusing on making the following three *"good health enablers"* as much a daily habit as brushing your teeth and showering. Healthy eating, thinking and physical exercise habits when formed at a young age carry over into adulthood.

## A. Making Intelligent Food Consumption Decisions

*Favor unadulterated food over heavily processed or refined varieties.*

Far too many foods today contain unnecessary additives, such as preservatives, colorings and flavor enhancers that may be harmful to your body. [Heavily processed foods (i.e., chips, dips, mass distributed baked goods and many breakfast cereals) are among the worst offenders.] Therefore, try to stay away from products containing too much of anything (especially, salt, sugar and fat) that are designed to appeal to the masses. Although the aforementioned ingredients are not bad for you in moderation, if regularly consumed in large enough quantities, they can lead to undesirable health consequences. High salt intake has been linked to hypertension; overindulging in refined sugars has been associated with diabetes; and a diet rich in saturated fats has been blamed for heart disease.

The best weapon to guard against eating unhealthy is to educate yourself (read up on the topic) and pay close attention to food ingredient labels. What may appear to be a healthy choice at first glance may not be so. A can of vegetable soup advertised as non-fat, low sugar may contain almost your entire recommended daily allotment of sodium. What you originally thought was a one serving size container may actually be broken down into two or more servings, per the "Nutrition Facts" disclaimer, to understate the product's high salt content.

Don't feel compelled to become an expert on nutrition (unless you want to become a Registered Dietician) or pressured into adhering to a strict organic or vegan diet. Extreme positions have negative consequences. If you are overly restrictive with what you eat, you may end up pushing yourself to the other end of the spectrum – A steady diet of junk food, which will wreck your health. Err on the side of balance and moderation when it comes to your food consumption choices and you will be fine.

"You are what you eat!" (Don't take my word for it. There are plenty of reputable articles published on the internet and elsewhere that speak to this topic so you can make your own informed decisions.) Please consider adhering to the following food consumption tips:

- Eat as close to the earth as possible. The less man has done to it (the fewer the ingredients), the better. (I.e., Plain carrots over carrot salad or a baked potato over French fries.)
- Favor raw foods over cooked foods, particularly with fruits and vegetables. The heating process reduces their nutritional value and grilling can impart carcinogenic properties.
- Limit your sodium intake and don't add additional salt to food to reduce your risk of hypertension. (Hide the shaker.) Eventually you will taste the natural, hidden salt content in much of what you eat.
- Limit your intake of fatty foods, especially *saturated* varieties found in meat products. They contribute to high cholesterol levels. Fat from seeds, nuts and other plant products are desirable, as are fish oils.
- Drink milk over others beverage when you are still growing. It has high calcium content for forming strong bones.
- As you age, increase your intake of water. It is the healthiest selection for adults (zero calories and "cleansing") if you are eating right.
- Limit your intake of caffeine, most commonly found in coffee, tea, soda and energy drinks. Too much caffeine causes anxiety and restlessness. To become reliant on caffeine to wake you up every day is far from ideal. If you are living a healthy lifestyle, including getting enough rest and exercise, there should be no need to do so.
- Eating slowly is an effective aid in eating the right amounts. It gives your stomach enough time to tell your brain when your body has had enough. When in doubt, eat less rather than more. Over eating interferes with your ability to think clearly and creates complacency.

- Never say never to junk food. If your diet is overly restrictive, you may not be able to stick to it. (More on the relationship between good food and good health in Chapter 4 - Food/Essentials.)
- Don't regularly overeat, even with healthy foods. High caloric diets lead to weight gain no matter how active you are. This increases the likelihood of obesity, which leads to a whole range of illnesses, such as diabetes and heart disease.

## B. Developing a Sound Mind Through Healthy Lifestyle Choices

*Too much of a good thing over the long haul can be bad for you, whether it be relaxing, exercising or socializing. Balance is the silver bullet for thriving and combating burnout.*

Eating the right foods and keeping your physical body in top shape (strong arms, legs, back; heart) will be far less beneficial if you neglect your mind/thoughts … your internal source of "sunshine".

There is a tight bi-directional connection between mind and body. So much so, they are essentially one. You are what you think and do (both comprise your lifestyle). A poorly fed brain, from either a junk food consumption and or negative thoughts perspective, is unable to cope with life's everyday challenges. If you regularly eat right and think positive thoughts, you will unlock your brain's power and allow it to be your guiding force to attain and maintain good health.

Consider the following to attain and maintain a sound mind:

- Limit, within reason, your material possessions and don't overdo social engagements. The more stuff you own and more activities you participate in, the higher maintenance costs and more demands on your "battery recharging" free time. Quality not quantity should be the driving force between what to buy or participate in.
- Keep friends that share similar healthy lifestyle values. They will serve as a support network to ensure you don't stray too far from your goals.
- View the glass as half-full. Positive thoughts have beneficial health properties
- Be your own best friend. The inner peace provided by fully accepting and loving yourself will reduce your reliance on others, material possessions

and food/drugs for happiness. If you can't count on yourself, who can you count on?
- Don't smoke. It is an addictive and destructive habit. Cigarettes, cigars, pipes and chewing tobacco are all extremely harmful and have been proven to cause cancer. Since tobacco products are among the most heavily taxed items around, this should be an added incentive to pick another vice.
- Wear a protective helmet when riding your bicycle or engaging in certain sports. Your brain is your future! If you injury it beyond repair, you will regret it.
- Drink alcohol in moderation. It can lead to cirrhosis of the liver and other health issues when abused over time. And, don't drink and drive. You are putting your own life at risk and innocent others.
- Say "No" to recreational drugs (Marijuana, Cocaine, Heroin, Crack, painkillers, etc.) as there are documented health risks associated with their use. Some of the more hardcore varieties are extremely addictive and can wreak untold havoc on your brain and finances.
- Get plenty of sleep and go to bed early. Benjamin Franklin, one of our country's most successful Founding Fathers thrived in the 1700's by adhering to - **"Early to bed, early to rise makes a man healthy wealthy and wise"**. As an added incentive to comply, a friend of mine who ironically lives near Philadelphia firmly believes, "Not much good happens after midnight." Why try your luck?
- Exercise your brain by reading as often as possible (or performing mind games like crossword puzzles or Sudoku). The more you read, the more you learn. Over time, you will amass a large knowledge repository in your head that will become quite useful in a variety of settings.
- Travel to new destinations to expand your real-world experiences. Start by exploring local places, such as nearby museums, flea markets or cultural events within walking or biking distance. Travel and exploration is stimulating, liberating and educational, especially if you read about the destination beforehand. And, if you gradually expand your travel radius by car or rail, you do not need to incur costly air or hotel expenses.
- Develop a strong relationship with God or a higher power. Through prayer, fellowship and adhering to the teachings of your religion, you will be rewarded with spiritual growth, inner peace and the ability to forgive – All necessary traits to help you make better sense of the many "challenges" you will face in the future and to provide you with the power to stay on the right path during tough times.

- Carve out time for yourself each day (alone time) to recharge your inner battery. Although this is essential when you have a family and are giving so much to others, it is important at any age to escape the "daily grind". If you need a break from studying, why not take a 20-30 minute walk and reflect on how you are feeling, where you are heading and where you need to be?
- Get into the habit of creating and maintaining a prioritized task list with to-do's. It will help you focus on accomplishing what is most important and goes a long way in ensuring you do what you intend when it counts most. Many people find that without a task list, they have trouble sleeping at night as they try to recall what needs to be done the next day, week or month. If you reduce your thoughts to writing, you should have a clean mental slate before your head hits the pillow.
- Don't become accustomed to cutting corners. You don't want to be sorry for what you didn't do. Doing "the best you can" day in and day out, with regard to **all** endeavors produces positive results and reduced stress levels. Obtaining a "C" grade in an advanced math class (i.e., Algebra, Trigonometry or Calculus) may be cause for celebration if you studied hard for every test and the subject was difficult for you to grasp. However, if you are gifted in the subject and received the very same grade, because you didn't study enough – How should you feel knowing that an "A" or "B" was within reach?
- Believe in yourself. If you don't, who will? Deposit each and every one of your past successes, no matter how small, into your confidence reserve. Success begets success and inspires you to call upon your vast array of personal knowledge (also contributed to by your failures) to overcome the many challenges that are sure to surface in the hours, days and weeks ahead.
- Know your strengths and weaknesses like the back of your hand. Realize though, you are much better served further developing your top strengths/talents than spending similar time trying to fix your weaknesses/shortcomings. ("Strengths Finder 2.0", Tom Rath, 2007.)
- Keep stress to manageable levels. Although some stress is beneficial, too much long term exposure can be devastating. A wealthy entrepreneur I got to know well suffered a massive heart attack at 48, without any prior warning, despite being a strict vegetarian, non-smoker and casual drinker. His only vice – He was a self-proclaimed workaholic, often putting in 18 hour days and 100 hour weeks like they were a badge of honor even though he had a young family at home. He was lucky to survive, but had to sell the successful business he built from scratch as a young immigrant to prevent

another occurrence. I can't help but think what the outcome may have been if he backed off work a bit and made time to exercise regularly.

## C. Establishing a Regular Physical Exercise Routine

*When you are too sedentary, you have one foot in your grave.*

Physical exercise allows our bodies to grow and remain strong … and it produces a fruit of sorts called happiness! It's difficult to be content without a healthy, pain-free body.

What exercise routines should you adopt? Those you enjoy doing. If you select something like running, but find it too monotonous or socially isolating, you will not stick with it. What good is merely thinking about working out? Pick an exercise program you like and results will follow.

Many fitness experts believe the ideal workout consists of thirty minutes of cardiovascular (anything that gets your heart racing), coupled with weight and flexibility training, three times a week. Cardio routines like running, swimming and biking keep your heart in shape. Lifting weights strengthens your muscles so you can perform every day activities easier and forms strong, denser bones supporting your entire frame. And, stretching (i.e., being able to touch your toes, or at least come close) and performing yoga type positions mitigates the possibility of damaging your muscles and tendons.

Don't be discouraged if your weekly workouts fall short of the "ideal". Some exercise is better than no exercise and there will be times in your life when other priorities take precedence … some of which will entail a workout in their own right, like participating in organized athletics which I highly recommend to build discipline and confidence and teach good sportsmanship.

In between your personalized workout routine (don't hesitate to consult a sports coach, team trainer or PE instructor for specific exercises), stay active and consider the following:

- Walk whenever you can, including to school. A brisk walk is as beneficial to your health as running without the wear and tear on your joints.

- Riding your bicycle is another excellent low impact activity that serves as a fun and fast way to get from Point A to Point B until you learn to drive.
- Choose stairs over escalators or elevators. The extra movement makes a difference in your overall health. (Corporate Wellness programs recognize this by encouraging participants to wear pedometers throughout the day to count their total steps.)
- Stretch your body frequently. Besides improving your ability to concentrate and reducing the occurrence of repetitive stress injuries (like Carpal Tunnel Syndrome), well stretched muscles, ligaments and joints are less likely to be damaged in an unexpected fall/accident.
- If you don't play organized sports at school, join a local club or league that allows you to channel your extra energy into something physically productive. The YMCA, Martial Arts pay-as-you go academies and County run Golf facilities all have programs that are good outlets for blowing off some steam.
- In lieu of spending time on the internet after school visiting social networking sites, tweeting or maintaining your Avatar, go outside and play the old fashioned way! Shooting "hoops" in the driveway, tossing a Frisbee with a friend or practicing your golf swing at a local park or driving range, will clear your head and feed your body.
- Turn common chores into exercises. Vacuuming carpets, washing/waxing cars or landscaping the yard (cutting the lawn, trimming bushes or weeding a garden), if done at a rapid pace has associated health benefits and will provide an immediate sense of accomplishment you can easily see, touch and feel.

In summary: Exercise regularly, whether it means walking, running or simply lifting weights. Exercise is an important component to good health, but it is not the most significant of the big three health enablers. If you don't eat right and achieve a sound mind through a balanced lifestyle, all the exercise in the world is not going to mean a thing. Take a holistic approach to caring for your body and with a bit of luck your mental and physical attributes will take you to great heights.

Remember – You are the most important income-generating asset you will ever possess. With a sharp mind and fit body, you will be able to study better and make more intelligent investment decisions (discussed next) when it counts the most so your personal foundation is rock solid and can one day accommodate a sturdy frame and quality roof.

# CHAPTER 3

## Investment Vehicles

*The earlier you start saving, no matter how small your deposits, the better off you will be thanks to the "magic" of compounding interest.*

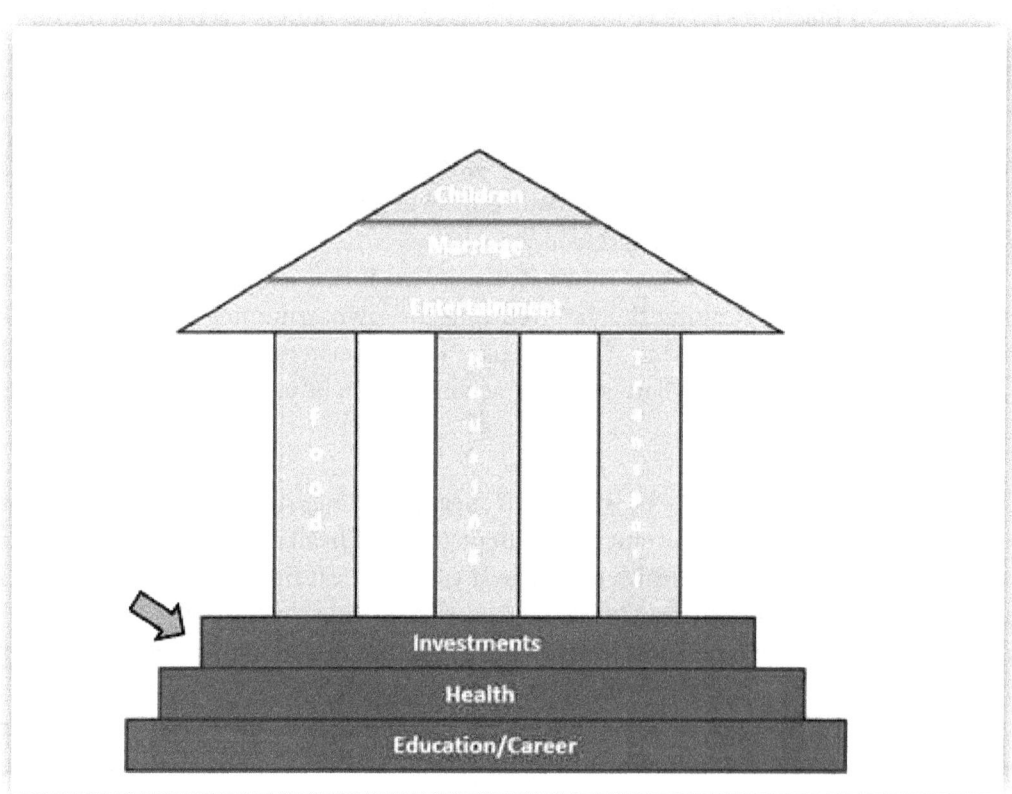

Building & maintaining EFI by managing your "spend"/focus on your investments.

## A. The Importance of Prudent Investing

What does intelligent and well calculated investing have to do with your savings success and Early Financial Independence? About as much as a home's foundation ensures the stability of the entire structure. Following sound age or life-stage appropriate investment principles will preserve *and* grow your hard earned money.

You can't retain the value of saved money (due to inflation) unless you wisely invest it. Stashing all your extra cash at home in your mattress, under a floor board or in a well-anchored fire-proof safe is risky in more ways than one. If your home is burglarized and the money stolen, odds are you will never see it again. (Most home owner's insurance policies cover only a small portion of your cash loss, usually between $200 and $1000 depending on carrier and policy.)

Moreover, keeping large sums of uninsured cash at home is unprofitable. Even if your money is not stolen, you are still being victimized with each passing day or month! How can that be if you can account for every hidden penny? By failing to *invest* or grow your savings, you are depriving yourself of interest income and being harmed by inflation by way of reduced purchasing power. The growing part is at the heart of succeeding financially. Most people can't sustain themselves long term on pure job/work income alone due to age constraints, diminished skills and limited opportunities. If you are ever to retire at a decent age, at some point you must make your saved money work for you, generating income while you are at rest.

An **"Investment"** in the broadest sense is "The act of committing money … to an endeavor with the expectation of obtaining an additional income or profit." (Investopedia.com). However, not all investments are created equal. Some are much riskier than others and may result in the loss of all of your hard-earned principle (what you started with). Risk is a part of life and can never be totally eliminated even with private insurance coverage or government guarantees. It is inherent in everything we do and *all* investments entail some degree of risk, no matter how infinitesimal or exceedingly small. As a general rule: The more risk you take on, the greater your potential returns or loss.

For prudent, savvy investors **investing** is "… putting money into something with the expectation of gain that upon thorough analysis has a high degree of security of principle, as well as security of return, within an expected period of time. (Wikipedia.com) I LOVE this definition! It offers a simple four part test to properly evaluate where to place your savings: 1) Have you given the investment opportunity much thought? ("Thorough analysis" of risk versus reward) 2) Will you be able to get back what you started with? ("Security of principle") 3) Are you likely to receive some form of payment (usually interest) for the use of your money? ("Security of return") And, 4) When EXACTLY will your principle be returned to you along with the payment for its use? ("Expected period of time" as opposed to an open ended date, like "sometime next year")

If you answer "No" to any of the above questions, hold onto your money and explore other investment options. Failure to do so is akin to gambling/speculation, much like playing the lottery where the odds are overwhelmingly stacked against you. You have a better chance of getting hit by lightning than having your Pick 6 ticket match up with the winning numbers. Unless you have money to burn, park your cash in "smart" places.

In the interest of full disclosure – The remainder of this chapter primarily explores how to preserve or retain what you save, while slowly but surely growing it into something larger. Bad investments erode savings at an alarming rate. It can take 5 years to save 50K, and only days or weeks to lose the same amount in a risky investment, such as a random stock pick. In other words, if you don't know what you are doing, you can lose your money at a faster rate than it took to accumulate it. The vultures are everywhere, anxiously waiting to feast on your irresistible "carcass" of misplaced savings.

Note: This chapter does not address how to "beat the street" and make significantly more money with your money. I am far from an expert on investing. Although I have read several books and articles on the subject by widely acclaimed professionals (I.e. Warren Buffet, Jim Cramer and Suze Orman), I still don't know all I need to know about "high return" investment vehicles, some of which are quite complex. And, because investing is such a personal matter, there are no black and white guidelines or right and wrong steps to help clearly shape your decisions. Risk tolerances vary widely among individual investors and I tend to err on the side of being overly conservative. With that being said, don't hesitate to study the subject if it interests you. There are numerous publications and resources at your disposal that address personal investing in detail.

## B. "Risk Free" Investing - Essential in Your Early Years

The best type of investing in your early years is **risk free** investing. Risk free investing is as safe as it gets. As long as the United States Government is in existence as we know it today (a democracy) and solvent, 100% of your deposits will be returned to you even if your bank fails! (If the U.S. is wiped off the face of the Earth or can't pay off its debts, you have much bigger problems to worry about than your savings success and Early Financial Independence.)

The Federal Deposit Insurance Corporation (FDIC), an independent agency of the United States government, *guarantees*: All deposits up to a certain limit made in **certain investment vehicles at FDIC participating financial institutions** are fully protected and insured. "Since the FDIC was established in 1933, no depositor has ever lost a single penny of FDIC-insured funds." (www.fdic.gov)

What is a qualifying "investment vehicle"? Savings/Checking Accounts, Certificates of Deposit and Money Market Accounts are all covered by FDIC insurance. US Treasuries like Savings Bonds are technically not included, but are warranted by the full faith and credit of our Federal government and are also essentially risk free in terms of receiving your "loan" back. Although, qualifying investment vehicles, pay lower rates of return than other options, take comfort in knowing they do a fantastic job preserving your principle investment and growing it over time thanks to regular interest payments.

**Savings/Checking Accounts** pay you interest (a fee paid by a bank) for the short term use of your deposited money. The interest is paid as a percentage of your deposit over a certain period of time, usually by month or year. (Wikipedia.org) The major difference between a savings and checking account is you can withdraw money more frequently and conveniently from the latter (via checks) and as a result are paid less in interest for this increased level of service.

A savings account is the best place to start investing until you accumulate a comfortable cushion of cash you don't need for anything else in the short term. You can open one up with a very small deposit and make frequent cash withdrawals from it (up to a certain maximum per month) without any assessed fees or penalties. And, just like the next two higher paying, but more restrictive class of accounts we will be exploring (CDs and MMAs) - A savings account introduces you to the wonderful world of compound interest.

Compound interest is "interest computed on the sum of an original principal and accrued interest." (Merriam Webster On-line dictionary) In other words, it is interest on your interest plus interest on your original deposit (principle). When you let your money accumulate and compound interest over a long time period, it increases more than you can imagine and can make you very rich.

An extreme, but commonly cited example: "The $24 paid by the Dutch to the local Indians for Manhattan Island [in 1626], if it had been invested at five percent interest, would today be worth more than **$2.2 billion**."(Best Steps.com) [Also, if you save 100K by age 30 and receive the same interest rate, it will grow to approximately 800K by age 73 when you are in retirement.]

The "Rule of 72" further substantiates this by providing an excellent estimate of how long it takes money to double at any interest rate. Simply divide the interest rate into the number 72. Five percent (5%) yearly compounded interest for the life of on an investment (deposit size not important), divided into 72 (72/5) equates to 14.4. This means it takes approximately 14.4 years to double your money at five percent interest, the same rate used in the Manhattan land purchase example. How much doubling would occur with the initial $24 in 389 years by say 2015? Answer: There are roughly 27 doubling periods between 1626 and 2015 (389/14.4 = 27.0129). According to the rule of 72 and some basic math, the initial investment would be worth around 3.2 billion dollars in 2015. And all it took was patience, capital preservation (not invading the principle) and the magic of compound interest.

**Savings account tips:**

- **Open a savings account as early in life as possible.** The sooner you get started, the more time the law of compounding interest will have to grow your money.
- **Shop around for the best interest rate before opening your account.** Rates vary widely and banks looking to expand their business usually pay more to lure depositors. Tip: Don't get hung up on daily versus monthly or yearly compounding. If you compare Annual Percentage Yields (APY), the compounding effect is already taken into account for you to compare "apples and oranges".
- **Make frequent deposits to reinforce the importance of saving/investing so it becomes a habit.** As an added benefit, the disciplined action of placing your money in the bank makes it harder to spend (must withdraw first after contemplating the decision), thereby minimizing the temptation to make impulse purchases.
- **Don't withdraw money unless absolutely necessary.** Doing so harms the exponential growth engine of compounded interest. (Less money to pay out interest on.) Leaving your initial principle intact could add hundreds of extra dollars to the account by the time you are ready to transition to another higher paying investment vehicle. And, when you eventually transition to another investment (i.e. Certificate of Deposit or Money Market), because you have a large enough initial deposit or can afford to tie up your money longer term - Resist the urge to spend some or all of it as a reward for having earned so much interest.
- **Don't close your original savings account!** Even though you may need all of the deposited funds to pay for college, keep a small balance in there to serve as a reminder you will one day be able to save again.

**Certificates of Deposit (CDs)** pay you a *set* rate of interest that is higher than you would earn in a savings or checking account, "in exchange for lending the institution money for a predetermined length of time" (Beginnersinvest.about.com)

A guaranteed, fixed rate of interest at a higher percentage yield than a savings or checking account is appealing, but only if you don't need the money within the pre-determined length of time (before it fully matures). If you attempt to withdraw your money prior to the CDs' maturity date, you will be assessed a penalty, usually in the form of forfeiting earned interest

"Maturities on certificates of deposit can range from only a few weeks to several years with the interest rate earned by the investor increasing in proportion to the time his capital is tied up in the investment." (Beginnersinvest.about.com) If you don't need your money anytime soon, commit it for longer periods (3 to 5 years) utilizing laddering techniques with staggered maturity dates to maximize returns and increase liquidity.

The major advantage of a CD - You can calculate your expected earnings at the outset of the investment with absolute certainty. The major disadvantage - You temporarily lose access to your funds so it is not as liquid as a savings or checking account.

**Money Market Accounts (MMAs):** In some respects, offer the best of both previously discussed risk free investment worlds. An MMA is FDIC insured, highly liquid (no maturity date) and "pays a fluctuating interest rate that, on average, is higher than the interest rate on ordinary savings accounts. However, a certain minimum credit balance must be maintained in an MMA, and only a limited number of checks can be written on it in a month ..." (businessdictionary.com) Note: It is also referred to as a "Money Market Deposit Account" (MMDA) and should not be confused with a Money Market Mutual Fund, which is not an insured deposit and considered riskier investing.

"Money market accounts are set up so you can readily access your funds without penalty. The price for this convenience is usually a lower yield on your investment ..." when compared with CDs. (Beginnersinvest.about.com). On the additional plus side, depositing money in a money market is as easy as depositing cash into a savings or checking account and your cash is immediately available for alternative investments. Be aware banks will often tease you with a high initial MMA interest rate. But, because the rate is not fixed, they often lower it after a certain time period (usually when the introductory period ends in 1 to 3 months). It pays to check the interest rate periodically and ask for a better rate if it is not as competitive as others in the area. Banks bet on the fact you will lose sight of what they are paying you, resulting in higher profits for them at your expense.

When you are living independently after college or graduate school, your first monetary goal should be establishing an emergency cash fund of 3 to 6 months of living expenses to pay for rent, food, utilities, transportation and other costs should you lose your job. As long as you meet the minimum deposit, a MMA is a great place for creating such a fund. And, you can automatically link it to your primary savings/checking account. When you reach a certain primary account balance, an automatic transfer of "x" dollars is sent to your higher paying MMA. When the MMA gets too big, you can open a CD with the extra money or explore Treasuries.

**United States Treasuries** are broadly defined as "government debt issued by the United States Department of the Treasury." There are four types of marketable treasury securities: Treasury bills, Treasury notes, Treasury bonds, and Treasury Inflation Protected Securities (TIPS). (Wikipedia.com) Although there are major differences between the four treasury types ... a topic for another day ... The most popular seem to be T-bonds, a long term investment which people often receive as gifts to celebrate their birth, baptism or high school graduation. "The money paid out for a Treasury bond is essentially a loan to the government. As with any loan, repayment of principal is accompanied by a specified interest rate. These bonds are guaranteed by the "full faith and credit" of the U.S. government, meaning that they are extremely low risk (since the government can simply print money to pay back the loan)." (investorwords.com)

In summary, although the interest rates provided by savings/checking accounts, CDs, Money Markets or Treasuries are low in comparison to other investments, your money plus more (namely, interest) will be there for you when you need it the most. While still in school or starting your first full time job, capital preservation should be your ultimate focus. The money you place in these accounts will inevitably be used to pay for unavoidable expenses to better yourself (i.e., educational costs) and is not excess you can afford to lose. When you can't afford to lose money, parking your savings in risk free investments is the only way to go. Never take on more risk than you can afford.

## C. Riskier Investing – When You Can Afford to Lose!

When you accumulate a comfortable cushion of risk free investments, financial planners strongly encourage you to risk a certain portion of it in pursuit of higher gains outpacing inflation. If your investment earnings don't keep pace with inflation, which is usually the case with "risk free" options, you are technically losing purchasing power with each passing day. In other words, your saved money, no matter where it is placed, becomes worth less with time by virtue of not earning interest that is on-par with the rate of inflation (the % a common basket of consumer goods increases from one year to the next).

To neutralize the effects of inflation on your savings, you must take on some risk. Safe investments pay out very little so financial institutions can make money off your money. They are, in essence, taking on the risk for you with your money and that is why they (and not you) are rewarded well for the loan. Capitalism does not reward zero risk! If everyone were guaranteed a high rate of return on a legitimate investment, everyone would want "in" ... which in a free market economy would drive down the return rate as only a limited amount of funds are typically required for any endeavor.

How much risk should you take on to potentially earn a higher rate of return? It's up to you and your individual comfort level. There are plenty of low, intermediate and high risk investment options available to you. Your job is to study the pros and cons of each, with the assistance of a trusted financial advisor, and make informed, well calculated decisions as to what investment strategy you should pursue that is appropriate for your age and life stage. And, there is no need to be mutually exclusive with your selections. You can and should spread your exposure over *all* three levels of risk with perhaps 50% of your portfolio committed to low risk options (i.e., Money Market Mutual Funds), 30% intermediate (index funds mirroring the S&P) and 20% high risk (individual stock picks).

**401(k)** - The best place to start a balanced "riskier" investment strategy is in your employer-sponsored 401(k) plan. A 401(k) is a retirement account that places the burden on you the employee to save for the day you "hang up your hat" for good, because you are either too old to work or think you have saved up enough to carry you through death.

In return for you managing your own retirement money and making tough investment decisions where you absorb all the risk, your employer will usually match your contributions up to a certain amount. You must take advantage of this benefit - no matter what you need to do to get there! Why not accept this free money? Equally attractive - Your contributions are subsidized by the government. You don't currently pay federal and state payroll taxes on 401(k) contributions (same applies to your employer) and all interest and dividend income is allowed to grow untaxed until you need it.

The major downside to a 401(k), you can't withdraw funds without a penalty until you are 59 ½ years of age so be reasonably sure you will not need the money until retirement.

Also, many financial experts advise against taking on too much risk in this account (like investing in part or exclusively in company stock), because you can't write-off the losses on your tax returns should you need to re-allocate your holdings.

Saving for your retirement is extremely important! There will come a time you can't work anymore and there are few guarantees in life, social security income included. Create your own destiny. Max out your 401(k) plan as soon as you can with the understanding it may take some time to do so as you are paying back student loans and or creating an emergency cash reserve.

**Individual Stocks** -To a large extent, riskier investing is on par with gambling since you are essentially betting on the uncertain outcome of a corporation or marketplace. If the odds are not stacked in your favor, don't put your money at risk. That is why I don't recommend individual stock picks (ownership in a company). If a company is not transparent, truthful or making the right management decisions, you pay the price by way of decreased stock values. Or like the former Enron Corporation, your entire stock could become worthless if the company you invested in files for bankruptcy protection, because they can't pay their bills.

With individual stocks, you must stay on top of things by dedicating at least one hour per week researching/re-examining the fundamentals of *each* of your current holdings. You can't sit and hold long term anymore. The market is too dynamic as General Motors can attest to. Diversity and balance is now the name of the game. Owning 20 to 30 different stocks across several different industries is often the recommended course of action for maximum protection. How can you own so many stocks if you don't have the time to manage them on your own? The answer: Through a Mutual Fund.

**Mutual Funds** – Are extremely popular. They are diversified, professionally managed and convenient, saving precious time from having to stay on top of it all. "A **mutual fund** is a professionally managed type of collective investment that pools money from many investors to buy stocks, bonds, short-term money market instruments, and/or other securities." (wikipedia.org). Funds are classified by their principal investments. A money market fund invests in money markets, bond funds in fixed assets, stock funds in stocks/equities and hybrid funds, a combination of the aforementioned. Another classification of funds worth purchasing, because they are so powerful and cost effective are Index funds. "An index fund or passively-managed fund seeks to match the performance of a market index [such as the S&P 500 index] while an actively managed fund seeks to outperform a relevant index through superior security selection." (Wikipedia.org) Most fund managers fail to consistently outperform the major indexes, while charging you a premium fee in the process. Avoid high fund fees and select a solid, reputable low cost index fund you can set and forget for a while.

**Real Estate** – Primary homes are not a true investment unless you rent a sizeable portion of it to a tenant. Homes depreciate with time if you don't update/modernize them and are best viewed as assets, anything than can be sold for money to offset liabilities/debts. (More on this topic below in section E. "False Investments (Fools Gold".)

Second homes, however, especially multi-family units are investments if they generate monthly rental income in exchange for their use. Pick premium locations, such as those near train stations, downtown shopping districts or schools, so demand is high even in recessionary times. Don't purchase vacant land. Owning land with no dwelling on it is a speculative investment since you only realize a return if and when you sell it. And until you do, you must fully bear all associated carrying costs, like yearly property tax payments, extra insurance fees and mortgage/home equity interest expenses. Furthermore, although your final negotiated land sales price may be higher than what you paid for it, you can't calculate a profit until you take closing fees, broker commissions and other miscellaneous transaction costs into consideration.

## D. Key Investment Principles to Accelerate EFI

- **Pay off your debts *first* to maximize your future savings potential!** Debt is more expensive than most reasonable investments are lucrative and over the long haul it is hard to make ends meet when you have a high debt load. Borrowing costs (i.e., the interest rate on student loans, car notes, credit card balances, home mortgages, etc.) are typically higher than what your extra cash could earn in risk-free investment vehicles. Therefore, it usually makes sound financial sense to fully repay your loan obligations as soon as practically possible. The longer it takes to satisfy your debt, the more you end up paying in interest. The adage of "paying yourself first" is only applicable if you are debt free or your borrowing costs are less than what you could earn with your extra cash elsewhere. Always ask yourself before investing – Is there a better use for my money, such as more quickly eliminating my debt?
- **Listen to your "inner voice" *before* investing.** Your first impression or gut reaction about something, also known as intuition, is usually more accurate than hours of deliberation. Emotions and over-analysis may convince you (or trick you) to go down the wrong path. You may decide to pull the trigger on a course of action, because you are so heavily invested in it from a time perspective and feel uncomfortable walking away with nothing to show for your effort. You are always better off cutting your losses early then incurring bigger ones later on. Schedule quiet time with yourself. You may be surprised what you hear.
- **The saying "If something sounds too good to be true, it probably is!" is as applicable to personal investing as anything else.** If some lone wolf offers you a guaranteed 10% rate of return on your money, when other like investments are in the 3 to 4%, range ask- Why the difference? (You could be about to enter a Ponzi scheme, where the funds of subsequent investors are used to pay for the fake returns of earlier investors.) Even if the highest paying option is a legitimate investment, such as an **insured** zero coupon bond, question - Who is insuring the insurance carrier, should it fail 10 to 15 years down the road?
- **Know your limits!** A false sense of confidence is the worst type of confidence. For example, if you don't fully understand the difference between "call options" and "put options", don't use them. Although they can be effective tools in limiting losses or boosting portfolio returns, if you don't know how or when to leverage them - Sit on the sidelines until you do! Just because you know the lingo, doesn't mean you are ready to play. And, what works for others may not work for you. You need to know *your* individual tolerance for risk and

fully appreciate the potential downside(s) of a failed investment. If your tolerance is high, that is fine, but be sure to ask yourself *before* taking action. 1) How much can you afford to lose? And, 2) Over what period of time might it take to recoup that loss in either the same or different investment vehicle?

- **Be rational, not emotional about your decisions.** You may love a restaurant's hamburgers or catchy ad campaign, but if their fundamentals are weak (losing money for years) think twice before buying their stock. If they declare bankruptcy, you'll be caught holding the bag. You may convince yourself the restaurant is due for a turnaround and the seemingly low $2 per share price is a bargain because it reached a high of $25.00 three years ago. However, there is a reason it is now selling so low, and it can go even lower to becoming worthless (zero dollars per share).
- **Greed is a major reason inexperienced and experienced investors alike lose money.** Some people are hardwired to push for higher and higher rates of return, ignoring flashing "warning signs" along the way, because the pursuit of more money is so addictive and all consuming. Don't place too much emphasis on money, especially the type that comes fast and easy. Greed, like love, is blinding often turning off your reality/intuition sensors so financial heartbreak is more likely.
- **Past performance is no indication of future performance**. Just because a stock or mutual fund has posted impressive gains over the past few years, does not mean it will deliver similar results now and in the future. Consider the following before buying: Has there been recent turnover at the senior leadership or fund manager level? (Not all financial minds think alike and there are very few geniuses in the business.) Has the business or fund grown too large? Is this an organization or fund you really want to own?
- **Invest for the long term whenever practical!** The market does not always price stocks rationally in the short term (day, week, month or year.) High flying emotions, like unbridled fear or irrational exuberance, sometimes temporarily cloud our vision of reality (the fundamentals). Leave day trading to the professionals and thrill seekers, and don't sell the first moment your stocks, funds or other investments dip in value. Over time, they are extremely likely to bounce back.
- **Don't invest for the long-term when you might need the money in the short-term.** As there are usually penalties for prematurely withdrawing your funds. The converse is also true. Don't invest short-term when you will not need the money for a while. Why accept a lower rate of return in exchange for liquidity you don't need? Select a 1 or 2 year CD instead of a 3 month CD if the rates are much higher. Note: Shopping around for the best deal usually

pays, even if it takes a full hour comparing local bank CD rates on-line at such reputable sites as Bankrate.com. $10,000 locked up in the best one year CD offering an extra ½ of one percent interest could net you an additional $50.00 for your efforts. Not bad for one hour's worth of research. It takes a lot of coupon clipping to result in similar savings.

- **It's not a level playing field when it comes to owning individual stocks.** Insider trading (using private data not yet made available to the general public to make stock buy or sell decisions) still occurs despite it being illegal to do so, producing unfair profits for some. I owned a small biotech stock whose entire value was based on a promising drug in phase III clinical trials. Two days *prior* to the announcement that the drug was ineffective and all trials would be curtailed (meaning lucrative FDA approval would not occur), a massive sell-off occurred (triple the normal trading volume) driving the price down next to nothing. Was this mere coincidence?

- **Diversity is the name of the game!** Some financial advisors counsel against too much diversification saying it "dilutes your returns". Instead, they advocate holding only a few well researched stocks to maximize profits. This approach can be lucrative, but carries significant risks if you are not an expert in the companies you own and their corresponding industries. Unless you possess true insider's knowledge, you have no way of knowing what direction an individual stock is headed. What if you select the wrong stock? Or, your "cherries" turn into "lemons" before you sell them? Err on the side of caution and build a diverse portfolio so you are not devastated by a poor decision or two.

- **Well balanced portfolios permit some degree of high risk taking.** Although your overall investment mix may be conservative or moderate, you can still pursue some aggressive growth options. (Meaning taking on high risk in well measured areas.) If 10-20% of your portfolio is extremely risky that's fine, because the other 80-90% can carry you if you fail. Don't be too conservative, you may have regrets later. Aim high (assume a fair degree of risk) on a certain percentage of your holdings, as long as you can afford the downside.

- **Don't *completely* trust your financial advisor/firm.** Closely examine their motives and "follow the money" trail. You will discover, more often than not, their number one goal is to sell you products, usually complex ones like annuities, to earn commissions or bonuses. The more trades/churns they make on your behalf, the more likely they are to earn additional money for themselves. If they are "incentivized" to sell you products/services or to trade for the sake of trading – Do they have your best interests at heart? Forget about what the law might say about regulating their behavior and/or their mandatory code of professional conduct. Most people are in it for themselves and will look the other way when it personally benefits them, as long as the chances of getting caught are slim or the reward is worth the risk. Therefore, don't give anyone the ability to sell your individual stock (without you approving it first) via a power-of-attorney. Unless you are incapacitated and can't grant prior approval for each and every transaction, your financial planner and or their co-worker(s) may be tempted to abscond with your entire portfolio, which might represent decades or more of hard work and patience. Sometimes financial advisors with stellar reputations, turn out to be the worst offenders. (I.e., Bernie Madoff.) The cloak of purity makes it easier for them to hide behind and today's saints can be tomorrow's sinners due to changed personal circumstances.

- **Always factor your age into the equation when investing.** The more years you are away from retirement – the more risk you can afford to take. If you suffer major losses at a young age, you can ride out your original selections over time and wait for their prices to rebound again. However, when you are a few years away from retirement (walking away from the working world), you should not be heavily invested in stocks. I know retirees who during the start of the 2007/2008 recession were almost exclusively invested in individual stocks. When the value of their holdings plummeted, they panicked and sold what they could at large losses to prevent further damage to their portfolio.

# E. False Investments (Fool's Gold)

A lesson in appreciating the value of true investments over personal assets: To the untrained observer, the mineral pyrite (commonly referred to as fool's gold) resembles the precious metal gold. They are both shiny in appearance and yellowish in color. However, their similarities end there. Fool's gold is relatively worthless, while real gold holds tremendous value and is a hedge against inflation, political turmoil and economic instability and is regarded by many as a form of currency.

Although gold is not a true investment according to the four-part test explored above in Section A: "The Importance of Prudent Investing" and its price can fluctuate widely over time resulting in the loss of money - Unlike fool's gold, two things are certain with real gold: 1) With a little bit of luck, it can become worth more than you paid for it without having to do anything to preserve its value and 2) It will always be worth something beyond a negligible amount since it is not a common commodity and does not depreciate in terms of a diminishing useful lifespan.

Personal assets are a different matter and more akin to fool's gold despite having a high initial monetary value. Most things we buy for our own use (i.e., cars, boats or homes) do not qualify as investments, but rather assets. An asset is simply "an item of value owned", (http://www.merriam-webster.com) that is worth something and can be liquidated for cash. Therefore, it is included on personal balance sheets and can be used to offset liabilities in determining net worth ... all desirable features.

Unfortunately, assets cost money to hold even when you are not using them, because they require some degree of maintenance, service or upkeep. Try parking a car in a garage for a year without using it and see what happens to its tires and exhaust system ... Or, leaving a boat in salt water for the same time period without cleaning its bottom, intake valves and water lines. The same can be said for the damage that would occur by not heating or cooling a home and its contents for extended periods of time.

Another major downside of owning assets - They generally depreciate (become worthless over time), despite regular servicing. Everything has a life span. Metal rusts, plastic cracks and wood rots with age through normal wear and tear. Unless a car, boat or home is virtually rebuilt from scratch with replacement parts, it will cease having any real value at some point and will eventually be sold for salvage, junk or residual value.

In short, maintenance costs, annual expenditures (i.e., liability insurance, registration renewals and licenses) and depreciation are enough of a reason to classify personal assets as a **"liability"** in the non-technical sense of the word. [A liability is anything that is a hindrance or puts you at a disadvantage because you are responsible for them. (http://en.wikipedia.org/wiki/Liability)] Therefore, buy only what you need and take pleasure in using them to their fullest to make their carrying costs worthwhile. Don't justify their purchase by considering them investments when they are not.

Beware of the following top "fool's gold" investment opportunities. The first two on the list (already referenced above) are worth repeating for staying power.

- **Primary Homes** – Are a luxury. You can rent a modest apartment or someone else's home/condo without having to foot the bill for costly repairs or updates. Although the land (an investment) does not usually depreciate, the physical structure/dwelling (asset) will unless you spend substantial money on maintaining it. Updates such as a new roof, furnace, plumbing fixtures, bathrooms, kitchens, driveways, etc. are costly and their life expectancies roughly range anywhere from 15 to 30 years depending upon the quality of materials/equipment used and overall craftsmanship to build/install. If your home is not newly built, you may only be a few months or years away from big ticket repairs and improvements.

    Buy a home to live in because it will enhance your quality of life. Don't buy one to make money. If you pick a great location for your home (and it stays that way ... no guarantees) and you do virtually nothing to maintain it, you may very well end up receiving a profit when you sell it. However, a poor

to average location with the same level of almost zero maintenance, may net you a loss at closing with or without cost of inflation adjustments. (**Chapter 5** explores how you can get the biggest bang for your buck on housing outlays ... your most costly personal expenditure.)
- **Motor Vehicles** – Are a necessity if you live in the suburbs, but they all lose value over time, even the expensive ones. The moment you drive a new car off a dealer's lot, you lose money to depreciation. With all things being equal -Why would anyone pay the same price for an ever so slightly used car as a brand new one? And, although some models hold their value better than others, this does not mean they are an investment or even a good buy. Ask – Is the upfront premium paid to obtain a higher re-sale value vehicle worth it when it comes time to trade it in for another one? You may find the more you spend on a car, truck or SUV, the more you will lose in the end. It usually costs more to insure, service and repair most higher-end vehicles. (**Chapter 6** contains advice on minimizing transportation related expenses to maximize your ability to save.)
- **Get-Rich-Quick Schemes** - Are unethical and often fraudulent/illegal and should be avoided at all cost unless you want to go to jail. Although there are many different varieties of them, you are most likely to encounter the pyramid scheme ... A non-sustainable business model "in which people are recruited to make payments to others above them in a hierarchy while expecting to receive payments from people recruited below them. Eventually the number of new recruits fails to sustain the payment structure, and the scheme collapses with most people losing the money they paid in." (http://www.answers.com) Chain letters/e-mails promising riches if you send money to "x" people on a list and encouraging you to perpetuate the act by enlisting the help of others is one such example. If you are not supplying a real service or product, what are you getting paid for? Participating in any get-rich-quick scheme is akin to building your dream home on someone else's land in return for a handshake promise you will someday be able to purchase the land from them at a reasonable price. Don't be a sucker.
- **Leveraging Credit Card Debt to Make Money** - Credit cards should be used as a tool of convenience and no balance is a healthy balance! Some people say you should keep a reasonable rolling balance (debt level) if you have good credit to free up your money to earn more elsewhere. These same proponents may also encourage you to accept "teaser" zero or low interest rate loans in the hope these temporary funds can be invested elsewhere earning a higher return than your borrowing rate. This is dangerous advice. You can't consistently out earn the high interest rates credit card companies charge.

And, if the borrowing rates are uncharacteristically low – It is because in the short term, returns elsewhere are meager and or they are betting on you not being able to repay the loan in full when it comes due.

Save money by not paying credit card interest in the first place. Pay off your balance in full each month to avoid incurring borrowing costs associated with having debt. As a training exercise, pay cash for almost everything you purchase for a long stretch of time. This ensures you can afford the item/service and serves as a not so subtle reminder of just how expensive things are. When you see money leaving your wallet, it may cause you to think twice about buying something and curb future purchases.

In closing, an investment is anything that makes you money with some degree of risk associated with it. Learn to minimize those risks by selecting the right investment(s) at the right time of your life. There is a season for everything. When you are young and attending school full time, an FDIC insured savings account is the prudent place to begin. If you save early and often, you will likely stick with this good habit forever.

No matter what investment strategies you opt for when you get older, don't be overly conservative nor take on more risk than you can afford. Both are costly plays when the name of the game is **capital preservation** *and* **growing your savings to at least keep pace with inflation.** If you hide all of your money under a rock for safe keeping, you may one day discover someone else has absconded with it. Alternatively, if you entrust *all* your money to one seemingly "reputable" advisor (a big mistake) you may end up in the same shape.

Every day people lose their entire life savings to poor planning or investment scams, because they trusted one person too much, perhaps a successful certified financial planner, a close relative or trusted friend/neighbor. Don't put all your eggs in one basket and only place what you can afford to lose in "riskier" type investments.

You will work awfully hard over many years to save up enough money to attain EFI. But, the challenges don't end there. You will have to work just as hard, **if not harder,** to hold onto what you save as there are many pitfalls along the way, including but not limited to, your own intermittent greed and mistaking fool's gold for the real thing when your ego gets in the way. Fancy cars and luxury homes may impress others, but they contribute little to your overall financial health and can have unintended negative consequences.

Best of luck finding an investment style you are comfortable with that solidifies and continues to fortify your personal foundation as circumstances change throughout the passing years! (I'm still trying.)

# Phase II

The Middle Stages – Establishing a Sturdy Frame:

(Early Adulthood/ New Found Independence - Managing the Necessities)

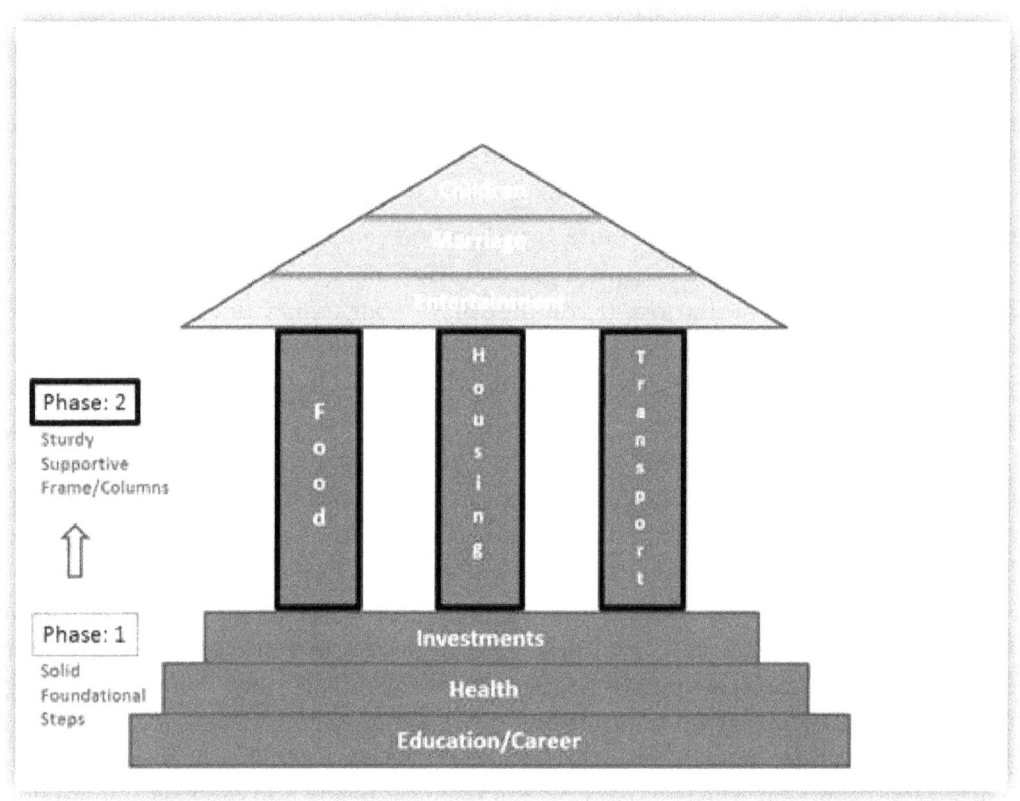

Building & maintaining EFI by managing your "spend"/focus on your personal frame.

Although creating a solid foundation is a critical first step in building a new home, it is arguably not the most important step. If you don't rest on top of a foundation a sturdy frame/skeleton (wooden/steel beams, floor joists, studs and roof rafters) providing proper support, shape and framework for the outer coverings and roof - Your home's strength and safety will be compromised. It may even collapse one day due to high winds or unusual seismic activity falling far short of a hurricane or earthquake.

Even if your Junior High through High School years were well spent laying a solid **"personal foundation"** for savings success (by focusing on education/career, health and basic investment vehicles), you are only a third of the way to achieving the primary goal of this guide. When you finally move out on your own and begin your life as an independent young adult (whether right after high-school, college or graduate school), your new found freedom comes with a substantial risk. Failure to properly manage expenditures associated with the "big three" basic necessities (akin to a building's frame), 1) Food/Essentials, 2) Housing/Shelter and 3) Transportation, will quickly derail your quest for EFI.

Two of the three necessities, Housing & Transportation, rank amongst the most expensive purchases you will ever make (their combined total cost often exceeds 50% or more of disposable income) and require you commit to signing long term contracts not easily terminated prematurely without large penalties. If you are not careful with your budgeting, you can get in over your head early in life and incur additional debt (beyond school loans) you may never be able to pay back.

Having to satisfy debt reduces your ability to save (sometimes anything at all) and the longer you delay saving, the longer you will be indebted to others and risk having your **"personal frame/skeleton"** collapse when facing such economic headwinds as the loss of a job or long term illness. The three chapters that follow guide you through making informed purchase decisions for costly necessities that will significantly mitigate this risk and contribute to you enjoying a stellar savings rate for years to come.

# CHAPTER 4

## Food/Essentials

*Although you must eat to live, be flexible with your food brand selections and do your homework before making purchases.*

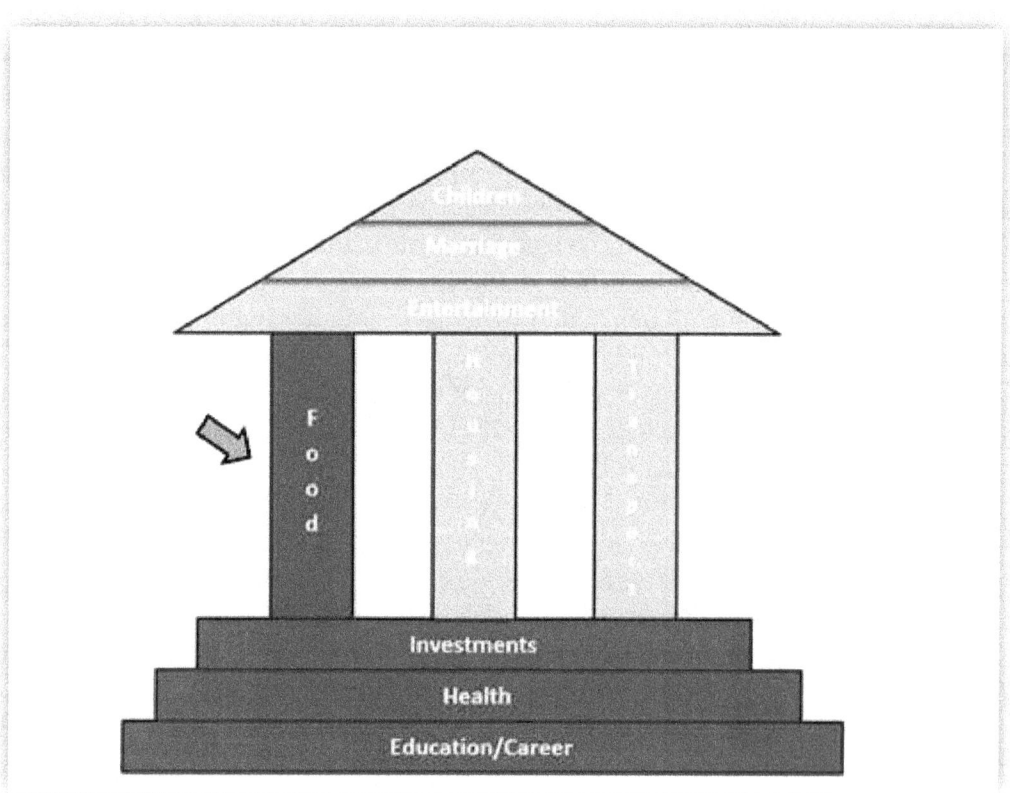

Building & maintaining EFI by managing your "spend"/focus on food/essentials.

## A. Brand Disloyalty

Loyalty to a particular food/essentials brand will cost you handsomely. Manufacturer's coupons, sales and special promotions are designed to get you "hooked" at the check-out line. Why? So you pay full price for an item, most of the time, for the rest of your life. If you believe you can't live without brand "x", you will pay more for it to stay within your comfort zone and continue reaping its alleged unique benefits. Manufacturers spend millions of dollars a year on flashy marketing campaigns to convince you of this.

Truth be told, most top brands are fairly similar in taste, quality or efficacy. I'm equally satisfied, for instance, with Heinz, Hunts and Del Monte ketchup products. (The same can be said for Colgate, Crest or Aim toothpaste.) Admittedly, I can see, feel and taste a small difference between ketchups, but only in a side-by-side comparison. Since variety can be refreshing, especially when it benefits you financially – Consider purchasing the lowest cost reputable product well in advance of depleting your current supply so you don't ever have to pay full price.

It's worth noting: A supermarket/retail chain's private label equivalent may be closely comparable in quality to the top brands and for much less money. (Keep an open mind and be willing to experiment.) There are little to no marketing costs associated with selling store brands. This savings is partially passed on to price sensitive consumers, who don't get caught up in fancy packaging and what others think about their consumption habits. However, not all private label offerings are a good value. Some are priced lower for reasons well beyond reduced marketing costs. With ketchup, the store brand may contain corn syrup instead of sugar, more water and fewer tomatoes (the star ingredient) to keep costs in check. Additionally, the tomatoes processed into store brand ketchup may not be as high a grade as those used in premium brands, which could translate into less taste and quite possibly nutritional value.

## B. 7 Ways to Save

Most adults know the basics when it comes to saving money on food and essential purchases. Very few are aware there are *many* options available to them to maximize their cost cutting efforts without turning the process into a full time job. Common sense, confidence and self-discipline are all you need to succeed. Below are seven time-tested ways to stretch your expenditures on must have items: (Always buy on sale, use coupons frequently, do comparison shopping, avoid impulse purchases, don't be afraid to negotiate, buy in bulk only when it makes sense and don't be lazy.)

1) **Always Buy On Sale** (By Being Brand Disloyal and More) - *Is a great way to get what you need for less with little effort.*

Odds are, every week shopping circulars for most major grocery stores in your area are delivered to your residence advertising their sale items for the upcoming promotional period. Each store's circular is designed to lure you in with loss leader specials (often posted on the first and last page) along with decent discounts for at least one item in every major food group. Large supermarket chains make money moving volume, not individual products. Their profit margins are razor thin, especially on food. Therefore, their main goal is to get you in their store and entice you to spend your entire weekly food/essentials budget with them in one trip. And, while you are at it, they hope you buy plenty of full priced items to make their promotional efforts worthwhile.

What the stores can't prevent you from doing is "cherry picking" the best sale items, stocking up on large reserves of them whenever practical and leaving the rest for another day. When chicken is on sale, buy some even though you may be in the mood for beef, pork or turkey. Odds are you will have the other meats stocked up in your freezer from previous sales and within a few days, you may opt for chicken after all. Next week, beef may be promoted allowing you to replenish your depleted stock … and the cycle goes on and on. If stores can play games, why can't you?

Main message: Buy *only* sale items whenever possible at one preferred grocery/retail store. Patronizing multiple stores in a week may further your savings, but is time consuming, places wear and tear on your car and wastes gas. If you shop almost exclusively for sale items at your favorite store (saving on having to run to multiple places), their sales cycle starts over again and you can almost always find what you need on sale. For instance, when you buy discounted pasta, get as many as the sale will allow and you have room to store. It will go on sale again in a few weeks, at the same store, usually just in time to purchase a new supply.

The perfect time to buy fresh fruits and vegetables is when they are "locally" in-season. Produce is generally more affordable when large supplies hit the marketplace during peak harvest times. And, perhaps the biggest benefit – The quality and taste of in-season produce is appreciably higher than out-of-season varieties. Ever eat a mealy apple in the winter that has been held in storage for a while that can't hold a candle to its firmer autumn cousin?

Timing is also extremely important when it comes to saving money on non-food items. Large retailers look to "unload" their unsold, in-stock supply of clothes and specialty items towards the end of their respective seasons to make room for new collections. In the late summer, for example, many stores significantly mark-down tee shirts, shorts and bathing suits (by as much as 75% or more) to make room for fall items such as sweaters, scarves and gloves.

Why not purchase swim gear then, when for most others doing so is just an afterthought? Likewise, why not buy that new sweater you need in January or February when retailers are gearing up for spring? If you religiously shop end of season sales, you will be rewarded with awesome deals!

Last thought on "always buy on sale" – The early bird gets the worm (Ben Franklin) so to speak, or at least the best selection. If you really need something on sale, buy it on the first or second day of the promotional period. [For exceptional savings on big ticket "teasers", like TVs, go the night before and ask that an exception be granted in selling it to you early.] That way you can increase the likelihood it will be in stock and in the widest possible range of colors and styles. Not all retailers provide "rain checks" when sale items have been depleted. (A rain-check is a promise to honor an item's sales price when its inventory is replenished, but only for a certain time period with maximum purchase count restrictions usually attached.) And even if they do, they are not applicable when a discontinued model is no longer on-hand.

2) **Use Coupons Frequently** – *They represent free or found money, but only if you genuinely benefit from the purchases they encourage you to make.*

A **coupon** is something that can be exchanged for a discount or rebate when purchasing a product. They are normally issued by consumer goods manufacturers or retailers in a paper based or electronic format to be used as a part of sales promotions and are widely distributed through mail, magazines, newspapers and the Internet. (http://en.wikipedia.org/wiki/Coupon)

The best part of coupons - They can be redeemed on already discounted items, greatly increasing your overall savings rate! My wife often spends $75 to $100 on weekly grocery shopping trips that would have cost $150 to $200 had she not almost exclusively purchased sale items and matched them up against coupons. You can save as much as you spend, netting a respectable 50% discount off your total food/essentials bill. Not bad for a few hours of work each month.

Caution is in order though. Coupons are designed to entice you to buy items, whether new products or long standing offerings, and require some degree of effort and coordination to redeem properly. If you don't carefully read their fine print, including expiration date, you could end up paying full price for something that doesn't qualify. A coupon, for instance, may only apply to the small box of cereal and not the large size. If you are accustomed to buying the latter, tossing anything else in your shopping cart may not come naturally. AND, your cashier may fail to inform you of the disqualification and that you paid full price.

You can reduce the chance of being overcharged for purchases by closely examining the point of sale system's monitor/display while your order is being scanned and reviewing your final receipt afterwards *while still in the store*. Both are essential to ensuring you got what you expected at the right price.

Coupon or no coupon, don't be lured into purchasing something: 1) for an insignificant discount, 2) you have no use for or 3) shouldn't be consuming at all. Thirty cents off a jumbo sized package of cotton candy meets all three criteria in my book. The last thing I need is another cavity in exchange for empty calories.

3) **Do Comparison Shopping** – *Vendors, retailers and salespeople often mislead you into believing you are getting good value in the name of increased profits or commissions.*
The best way to consistently receive good value is to do your "homework" (perform some degree of meaningful product comparison) before making even simple repeat purchases. A small mistake can easily become magnified when repeatedly made and could end up negatively impacting your pocket book *and* health.

Some people think "bread is bread" and "bigger is better". Without closely examining the label of a seemingly reputable brand, they toss the cheapest biggest white loaf or two in their cart and move on to the next shopping list item without any hesitation. And, they do this week after week, year after year.

Not all bread is equal. Some products contain *more* air, artificial colors/flavors, high fructose corn syrup, saturated fat and sodium than others, while offering *less* whole grains and fiber, which are essential to achieving and maintaining good health. Ask yourself after reading product/nutritional labels: Is the smaller package of bread actually denser (as measured in pounds, ounces or grams) than the larger one you are tempted to buy making the former a better value? Should you sacrifice some degree of quantity for quality? Are there significant health benefits to regularly consuming wheat over white bread? (Numerous studies seem to think so!)

In some cases, comparison shopping is practically unnecessary. When it comes to common commodities (i.e., bleach, vinegar, sugar, salt and flour) where product differences are minimal at best, a quick price and quantity check is enough to constitute due diligence. And, more often than not, the store or generic brand is the best bargain even when not on sale. Name brands with coupons usually don't measure up to no-frill store brand options due to higher overhead costs. Salt is salt isn't it? Why should you pay more for Morton's sodium chloride ($NaCl$)?

Your time is worth something. Don't over-compare sale items when the potential savings is small. Save your limited time and brainpower for larger, more significant decisions so you don't fall prey to the "penny wise, dollar foolish" trap.

4) **Avoid Impulse Purchases** – *And, you will be rewarded with savings almost every time!*

There is a huge premium associated with buying anything when it is most appealing to the masses. Cold bottled water at the beach, hot buttery movie theatre popcorn and cool "in-season" must have clothes at your local department store will all cost you extra. There is a price to pay for added convenience and the positive feelings associated with instant gratification.

As stated earlier, acquiring a bathing suit in the spring time in the Northeast can easily cost double the price of a comparable one purchased in late August. If you already have a good swimsuit heading into summer – Why not wait until the off-season to replace it with a newer one?

Other tips to avoid impulse purchases:

- Stay away from vending machines. Most of their selections are unhealthy and overpriced in relation to brown-bagging your own homemade snacks. (Just one vending machine trip a day, restricted to school or work, can add up to well over $400 a year and a few extra unwanted pounds.)
- Resist the temptation to purchase anything at or near check-out lines. You can usually get a whole lot more of the same or similar item at a discount in other sections of the store. Why not buy a multi-pack of gum in the candy aisle for roughly the same price as an individual packet?
- Don't grocery shop on an empty stomach. When you are hungry, you are more inclined to make irrational decisions. Like buying way too much of a perishable dairy product (not suitable for freezing) that can't possibly be consumed before it expires.

There is a season for everything and timing is extremely important in saving on food and essentials. If you are patient, flexible and disciplined, your ultimate reward for dealing with some discomfort will be extra dollars in your wallet.

5) **Don't Be Afraid to Negotiate** - *If you ask for reasonable price concessions, you will usually receive them.*

Although not all retailers are permitted to negotiate or bargain on the spot with you, most of the larger, nation-wide chains have price match guarantees or policies in place where they will beat the competition by x% if you present them with a more compelling advertised offer. The only way to realize this benefit is to research your purchase first and to remember to ask for something better if warranted. If you don't ask, you don't receive. It's that simple.

Only in rare cases will someone offer you a better price or more attractive deal on something without you asking for it. Sellers start the negotiation process by marking an item a certain price … the price they want you to pay, also known as the initial offer. If they lower their price just for you, without you asking to pay less, they will harm their profits and perhaps take home pay by leaving what's called "money on the table." If you remember one thing from this section, remember - **Successful sellers don't "bid against themselves" and are well adept at dealing with silence while waiting for counter-offers from buyers.** (A counter-offer is what a prospective buyer, like you, is hoping to pay for an item.)

If you walk away from a deal and head to the exit doors, your body language says, "I'm not interested or not ready to make a decision based on your initial offer." Many sellers spring into action at this point and offer a much better deal for fear you are going to buy elsewhere.

Small family owned businesses, flea markets and fresh produce stands are often excellent places to negotiate for food and essentials savings. They are usually much more flexible than larger corporate owned enterprises when it comes to carving out exceptions to policy as there are less people to go through to "get to the top". More often than not, my negotiation experience has been very favorable at these venues. If you ask nicely to *reasonably* "sweeten the pot", you will usually succeed. It's all about fairness (creating a win/win) and the merchant's willingness to help someone they like.

Other tips to negotiate savings beyond 1) simply asking for more in a pleasant manner, 2) picking the right location/venue and 3) walking-away from a deal:

- Ask if there is a coupon or special offer you are not aware of. Most store associates will go that "extra mile" to help you.
- Ask for group/bulk purchase discounts. Is there a better deal to be had if I buy more than "x" shirts, jeans or pizzas? Vendors usually have pricing tiers based on volume thresholds.

- Inquire if sales are more spectacular at other times of the year. This is most applicable to big ticket items like mattresses, furniture or electronics where a longer purchase delay may be worthwhile.
- Is there a special time of day items get discounted in mass? At many grocery stores, bakery items, rotisserie chickens and ready-made sandwiches are substantially marked-down at night when store traffic significantly lessens. Why not schedule your regular weekly shopping trip around this time to maximize savings?
- Does your supermarket's produce section have a discount rack with slightly blemished or overripe items? If not, ask a produce clerk if they can mark-down a qualifying item or two for quick sale. (Like bananas that must be eaten in a day or two.) The store would rather realize some revenue than zero revenue, as would occur with spoiled, tossed out produce.
- Is a frequent shopper or loyalty card available? You might be surprised how many establishments, like car washes, ice cream stores and car repair centers (for oil changes) offer the 10$^{th}$ item or service for free. And, they may only provide the card to customers who specifically ask for them.
- Local garage and estate sales can be a great place to buy non-food essentials such as dishes, cutlery, cups, irons, toasters, and other must have items to get started out at college or in your first apartment. Even paying top dollar at an estate sale for barely used furniture can be an exceptionally good buy. Sometimes "older" items are made better (finer craftsmanship) and out of higher quality materials than their more modern counterparts.
- If I pay by cash, will you provide an extra discount? Always save this for the very end. It hurts your position to bring it up earlier in the negotiation process. If the seller knows you will be paying by cash, they may make that a condition of their follow-up offer so they don't have to discount the item any further, leaving you with one less negotiation point.

Nothing ventured, nothing gained is great way to look at negotiating a better deal. If you don't ASK for additional savings, you will not receive them. What do you have to lose by trying? Nothing if you do it in a respectful manner!

6) **Buy in Bulk ONLY When It Makes Sense** - *Being excessive has its drawbacks in terms of spoilage, clutter and gluttony.*
   For non-perishable essential items, like paper products (towels, toilet tissue and napkins) that are excellent buys, buying in bulk makes perfect sense as long as you have the space to store them. If you are going to eventually use them all – Why not stock up when it is financially most advantageous to you?

Be careful with perishable items that your initial savings are not diminished by spoilage and that you are giving storage priority to higher priced items (meat in limited freezer space situations as opposed to bread). A large discounted bushel of tree ripened peaches may seem more appealing than a smaller sized container being sold at full price, but not if you lose 1/2 your purchase to rot. (Peaches, like pears, nectarines, plums, tomatoes and other fresh produce, ripen very quickly and at the same time.) Nine times out of ten, you will end up over-consuming bulk produce purchases (not necessarily a good thing) or giving them away to friends/family before turning bad. Why not purchase only what you need and gift what makes sense?

Almost everything has a shelf life or expiration date, including aspirin, vitamins, sun screen, canned food, dried beans, rice, pasta, cereal, frozen meat, refrigerated butter – You name it! Resist buying in bulk if there is a good chance you will not be able to use it all prior to its shelf life expiring. And, even when spoilage is not an issue, the nutritional value of food tends to diminish with age. A case of peanut butter, for example, that will take you 2 years to finish is a terrible purchase. Peanuts and peanut oil go rancid in 6 to 18 months depending on style/ingredients (all-natural versus preservative filled) and storage conditions. The supposed deal of the century will usually resurface in a few months, so show restraint.

7) **Don't Be Lazy** – *You reap what you sow (GALATIONS 6: 7-9).*
It takes effort to: 1) look for sale items, 2) clip coupons, 3) comparison shop, 4) avoid impulse purchases and 5) negotiate with sellers ... all proven ways to reduce your spend on food/essentials. In other words, it takes action and energy on your part to realize savings! If you are unwilling to do so, it's your loss – No one else's.

Additional ways to **earn**/reap savings:

- Pack your own breakfast, lunch and snacks to take to school or work. "Brown bagging" it, especially in the early years, will save you much needed money. A subsidized $5.00 lunch, consumed five days a week for a whole year, will cost $1250.00 for instance. You can pack your own healthier alternatives for half that amount using quality ingredients that are lower in sodium, sugar and fat.
- If you are a regular coffee drinker, brew you own at home. There is a large markup on coffee, regardless of where purchased due to the service component of the offering. A local fast food restaurant, deli or mini-mart may be more affordable than Starbucks or other premium brand, but none are a

better bargain than a cup of steaming hot Java prepared in your own coffee maker. (Pour some into an insulated thermos to take it on the go and it will stay hot most of the day.)
- Shop thrift stores. You will be surprised how little you pay for gently used clothing that usually supports a good cause. Infrequently worn items, such as holiday attire are especially good value as are toys, musical instruments, and sports equipment. This method of shopping requires more effort than frequenting department stores, where the selection in each brand/style is typically plentiful. (There is a cost to bear for the convenience of being able to try on in one visit multiple sizes/lengths of your favorite blue jeans to make a quick informed best fit decision.)
- Learn to cook. Restaurant food and takeout meals are costly and usually unhealthy due to high sodium, sugar and fat content. (Restaurants are more concerned with the taste of their food than your physical well-being.) If you can cook (not just talking making toast, boiling eggs and slathering peanut butter and jelly on bread), you can reduce your reliance on heavily processed or adulterated foods. Why not make your own soup instead of relying on a can? Your healthier version will cost much less and freezes well for future meals making the production and cleanup effort well worth it.

## C. Spend More On Healthier Food Choices - *A "penny saved may be a penny earned" (Ben Franklin), but not for long if made at the expense of good health.*
Nowhere is this principle more relevant than what you put "in" and "on" your body. Saving money is important, but not as important as your health and safety. Scrimping here and there at the expense of good health is "penny-wise, dollar foolish" (Saving small amounts resulting in greater future expenditures). You will pay for your indiscretions ... It's just a matter of when, not if.

You are better served spending more on healthier food choices like fresh produce, lean cuts of meat, whole wheat bread and low sodium selections. You will feel better, possess higher energy levels and save money over the long term when you invest in good health. Healthy eaters tend to have FEWER: 1) doctor's visits and resulting co-pays, 2) over-the-counter/prescription drug needs and 3) surgical procedures than those who eat junk food on a consistent basis.

The mindset of health conscious consumers is evidenced by: Selecting corn-on-the-cob or cut corn over fried corn chips to accompany a meal, choosing baked or mashed potatoes over potato chips or French fries and opting for more expensive "all-natural" peanut butter (just peanuts) over versions with added sugar, fat and salt. They also generally buy chicken breasts, London broil, pork loin and fish as their main sources of meat/protein. Chicken breasts are more expensive than other chicken parts, but are lean and relatively quick and easy to cook—so they offer a good cost to value tradeoff.

Health conscious consumers also regularly pass up on less costly high fructose sweetened drinks, like soda, for 100% fruit juice varieties. They learn to offset the additional cost by making water their beverage of choice, often with a dash of lemon or lime to spice things up a bit. Stay away from bottled water, especially those with designer labels. It is expensive and the plastic containers bad for the environment … And what's bad for the environment will eventually negatively impact you. Although tap water is your best bet to keep costs in check, make sure the source is safe. Better to spend a couple of bucks on bottled water when in doubt.

In terms of vitamins, consider spending more on brands that comply with "Good Manufacturing Practices" (GMP). GMP certified manufacturers have more stringent quality control processes in place than their non-GMP brethren. Why not pay a little extra for better quality and additional regulatory oversight?

Similar logic applies to generic medicine. Ask your doctor or pharmacist if generic brands are worth the dollar savings over well-established name brands. Some drugs are not easy to replicate. Therefore a particular generic drug may not be as potent or effective as the original patent holder's drug. They **should** be the same exact bio-equivalent, but this does not always hold true.

## D. Safer Non-Food Essentials

What you wear or use externally can be as important to your health and safety as what you ingest. Sacrificing quality for cost savings when it comes to footwear, for example, can result in back, knee and foot pain. Low-end sneakers do not contain the same support, cushioning and padding that more expensive, well-built models offer. Buy the best pair of shoes you can afford, within reason, and your body will benefit.

Entry level mattresses are often poorly constructed, containing fewer coils or layers of memory foam. Avoid the temptation to purchase them for extra savings. They are generally less comfortable than other models and may interfere with a good night's sleep. Without adequate rest your health with suffer. The average mid-range mattress and box spring set lasts for 7 to 10 years. Why cut corners on something you will use 2500 plus times? I'm all for saving money, but know where to draw the line. This comes with experience.

Where a product is made is as important as how it is made and could have safety implications. Some foreign manufacturers take bigger risks than domestic companies when it comes to instituting cost cutting measures, including using marginal supplies from disreputable vendors. My wife once bought a pair of slippers made overseas containing slip resistant rubber soles. The soles omitted a strong chemical odor that made our eyes tear when we examined them up close. After airing them out in the garage for a month, the smell remained so we discarded them to err on the side of caution. No telling what unapproved filler ingredients were used to conserve on more costly raw materials.

In conclusion, if you live and breathe the "7 Ways to Save" for food/essentials *and beyond* (i.e., for comparing/purchasing a college education, investments, cars, homes or services), you will not be disappointed! The savings you can reap for yourself are stellar. BUT ... don't "pinch pennies" at the risk of compromising something more valuable than money - Your good health. If saving money is your only guiding force, your personal frame might collapse. Just as using too few nails to secure a home's wooden support beams spells trouble, so can poor food and essentials choices.

# CHAPTER 5

## Housing

*Before purchasing or renting property, perform a total cost of ownership analysis to determine affordability.*

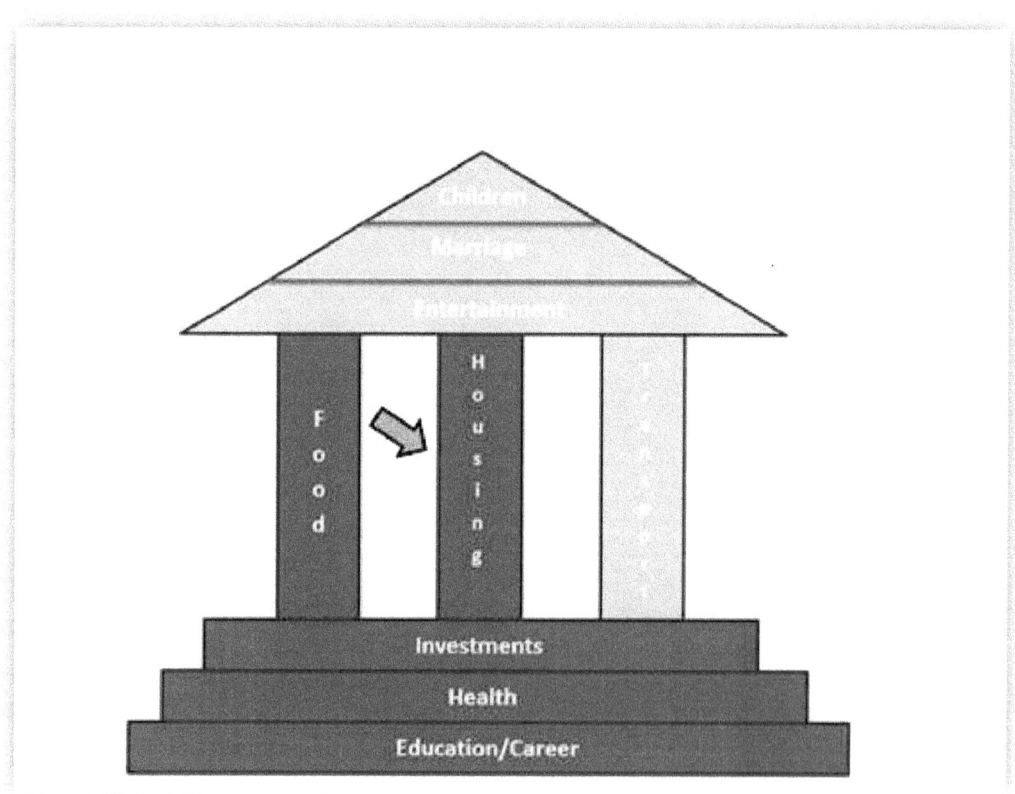

Building & maintaining EFI by managing your "spend"/focus on housing.

If you don't factor into the equation **ALL** of your likely direct and indirect housing related expenses, you could become a "prisoner" of your own home. A prisoner in the sense all or a substantial portion of your disposable income is "locked-up" in housing related expenses, preventing other necessary purchases or pursuits.

If this happens, you are said to be "house rich, cash poor" ... Meaning your living arrangements are financially all consuming and interfering with basic needs like putting food on the table, securing transportation to/from work and saving for a rainy day.

Since it's not easy reversing getting in over your head with owning real estate, because it is highly illiquid (can't be easily converted to cash in a short time frame) and entails substantial closing, transaction and transfer costs – Start off conservatively with housing commitments to ensure you are the master of your own domain. When your domain is the master, you are in for trouble.

Note: The term "home"/"house" is defined broadly herein as any place providing a safe roof over your head whether rented or owned. A single detached home is only one type of living arrangement. There are many other less costly "starter" options available to you that are more age/circumstance appropriate as you begin your journey to financial independence. Renting a room or studio apartment are two such options as addressed next.

## A. Renting – A Reasonable First Step

When done right, renting is a great way to transition to living on your own. It's almost impossible to become "imprisoned" renting a bedroom in a private residence or small modest apartment (like a studio design where you live and sleep in one room) until you can afford more. And, if you find a roommate to split costs with, you will save even more money and may be able to live in a nicer neighborhood closer to school or work.

Living at or preferably *below* your means is critical to long term savings success. If all you can afford is $500 a month for housing – You shouldn't spend more (overindulging on housing) hoping your salary will soon catch-up! Your goal at any age should be to live comfortably, not excessively, while saving as much money as possible to solidify your personal financial foundation. This is particularly crucial when you are fresh out of school and looking to build a first time safety net/cushion of cash.

When traditional home ownership is out of reach, resist the urge to rent an expensive apartment with perhaps the same amenities you enjoyed as a child. You should earn your way up the "housing ladder". No one owes you anything and expecting something for nothing is a dangerous entitlement mindset sure to disappoint. Create your own destiny and wealth by respecting your financial condition and **living consistently below your means.** (This is arguably the most important principle in this guide and simply means spending much less than you take in.) If renting is the way to go, avoid the temptation to impress others and secure a modest apartment.

There are many benefits to renting in your early years, when you don't have a spouse and kids in tow:

- *Your monthly costs are fixed.* - Making it easier to budget your personal finances. If the hot water heater, furnace or stove breaks in your apartment, your landlord is obligated to repair them at their expense.
- *You only pay for what you need.* - Why absorb the cost of extra space/square footage, such as a second or third bedroom, a basement or backyard when you don't need them? Why not continue to tough it out to some extent when a small upgrade in living conditions (i.e., from a shared college dorm room to small private one) is still seen as a win?
- *Apartments are virtually maintenance free.* - Affording you more time to focus on what matters most at this stage of life ... Like your career and dating. It's difficult to get promoted or find a soul mate if you are spending significant time with such basic upkeep as performing plumbing repairs, mowing the lawn and cleaning gutters.
- *There are no long term commitments.* - If given the choice, opt for a month to month lease as opposed to a one year rental period. The extra flexibility is nice if you decide to relocate for work, a love interest or to explore another community. Although you may be penalized "x" month(s) rent to break a lease, it may allow you to capitalize on a bargain too good to pass up ... Like your first home, when you have enough money for a large down payment and your career is established and stable.

## B. Owning - Often a Highly Desirable Second Step

There may come a time in your life when you seek more privacy, living space and or control over customizing your surroundings than an apartment can provide. Trying to pack two kids, for instance, into a standard two bedroom apartment can be challenging, especially if storage space is at a premium. Kids tend to accumulate more toys and clutter than adults and benefit immensely from having a garage and easy access to a backyard play area.

Additionally, owning a home provides for the accumulation of equity, a form of forced savings. The pursuit of equity is partially subsidized to the extent your mortgage interest and property taxes are deductible on your federal and state income tax returns. And, should your property increase in value (no guarantee it will, when factoring inflation into the mix), you are entitled to retain the appreciated portion when you sell. This holds true regardless of whether you own a single family home, duplex, condominium or cooperative.

Living the American dream via home ownership has drawbacks. The most obvious ones are the inverse of the previously mentioned rental benefits:

- *Monthly costs are variable and unpredictable.* - You never know when you might have to spend hundreds or thousands of dollars **unexpectedly** treating termites ($1000), replacing your furnace ($5000+) or dealing with water damage.
- *You typically pay for more space than you need.* - The average home consists of more "nice to have" luxury space than the average apartment and these extras are often underutilized. Case in point: The spare/guest bedroom accommodating visitors only a few times a year. Wouldn't an air mattress in the living room work just as well?
- *Maintenance efforts are quite high.* - It's your driveway, lawn and front steps. Should anything fall or grow on them, like leaves, snow or weeds, it's your obligation to remove them. Plus, maintenance extends to the whole interior as well. It's your flooring, ceiling and walls to repair and replace.
- *You are locked into the first three drawbacks for a much longer commitment period.* - The average home mortgage is 30 years while the average rental period is one year. Although all contracts can be broken, it is much more difficult and expensive to re-finance a mortgage or satisfy it in full through the sale of your property than breaking or re-negotiating an apartment's lease.

Before purchasing a home, the single largest expenditure you will ever make - Be sure you can afford *all* aspects of owning it over the long haul. How do you assess if you can afford a particular home? By plugging the total cost of home ownership figure into the expenses side of your Personal Income Statement and doing the math. (See Appendix B for sample statement) Businesses use Profit & Loss statements to determine the overall health of their cash flow and profitability for a slice in time. Shouldn't you do the same?

Column A in your Income Statement should contain a list of all monthly income/revenue sources, such as *net* pay from your job and interest/dividend income from your investments. (The value of your assets should not be factored into purchase decisions unless you plan to liquidate/sell them.) Column B is where you detail all monthly expenses, liabilities and obligations, including but not limited to your housing costs. If column A (income) minus B (expenses) is a positive number, you are operating "in the black" or living within your means. When the reverse is true (expenses exceed income) you are operating "in the red" and living above your means, signaling you can't afford your lifestyle.

Evaluating whether or not you can afford a given home can't be done in a vacuum without consulting your Personal Income Statement. An ownership analysis that *only* measures housing related expenses against your current income stream, is misleading as it provides a distorted picture of affordability as evidenced by the below example.

If your dream starter home costs $3000.00 a month (including mortgage payments, property taxes, homeowner's insurance, utilities, garbage disposal fees and maintenance outlays for normal "wear and tear") and your take home pay (money you get to keep after taxes) is $4000.00 – Do you have enough information to decide if you should purchase it? Absolutely not!! (And, don't be misled by the apparent $1000 in extra cash as this is not an accurate number.)

Even if you are fortunate to *not* have other big ticket financial obligations (like student loans, car payments, credit card debt, childcare expenses, etc.), you still have other ongoing, routine monthly expenses you must budget for. How about expenditures for food, tolls, gasoline and dry cleaning? What about the need for occasionally reaching into your pocket for new clothes, haircuts, medical insurance co-pays and oil changes? These aforementioned living expenses can easily cost $400 to $500 dollars a month. But, the good news is they are reflected in any well-constructed Personal Income Statement for optimal visibility.

When it comes time to make a final decision on your prospective dream home, a few hundred dollars in savings each month may not be enough to accomplish other important objectives, such as creating/maintaining an emergency cash reserve, maxing out your 401k plan contributions and saving for a replacement car. If you bought the home in this scenario, you would technically be living within your means (operating "in the black" by saving around $500 a month or $6K per year). However, you are best served **living well *below* your means,** loosely defined as spending much less than your take home pay and other income streams allow for in relation to your debt load for accelerated savings, which bring you one step closer to Early Financial Independence.

## C. Living Below Your Home Ownership Means By:

Obtaining a sensible mortgage, not viewing your primary residence as an investment and not caring what others think about your living arrangements.

### Obtaining a Sensible Mortgage:

A mortgage is a written promise to pay back a specified loan amount with interest on a monthly basis over "x" years in return for the privilege of living in a residence. It is one of the most important documents you will ever sign. If you are unable to pay your mortgage on time, the financial institution holding your note/loan can evict you from your home and foreclose on your property, potentially resulting in the loss of all or some of the money you paid towards the house. This remedy is provided for in all mortgage agreements and usually further stipulates that the person being foreclosed upon must bear all transactions costs associated with the forced sale. Bottom line: Your home is not legally yours until the mortgage is paid off in full.

Since a missed payment or two could land you in trouble: **1)** Make sure you can afford the monthly mortgage obligation, which often includes your town's property taxes. (The two figures added together can be quite large.) **2)** Stick with a conventional 30 year fixed mortgage or better yet, a 15 year fixed if you can handle the larger payments. No-money-down loans, variable rate loans or fixed periods greater than 30 years can land you in hot water. If you can't come up with a down payment of at least 10% of a home's purchase price, you are not ready to handle the financial responsibility of owning a home. Why pay a premium (usually via "points" or a higher interest rate) to prematurely occupy it?

Variable rate loans are scary. After a temporary teaser lock-in period, your payments can increase considerably. If interest rates shoot through the roof in the future, a 2K per month payment can turn into a 3K obligation. And, why pay interest for more than 30 years? At one point I recall banks hawking 50 year fixed rate loans. If you need to spread your payments out over an extra 20 years, shouldn't you consider a less expensive property or remain on the side-lines longer?

Additionally, don't listen to mortgage professionals and spend **28 to 36%** of your **gross** income on housing related costs. Or, similarly rely on their on-line calculators with special algorithms looking to limit your debt to income ratio to **40 to 50%**. Mortgage companies make more money in the form of additional interest income the more you borrow. Although they generally prevent you from borrowing too much to reduce the risk of a costly default/foreclosure, they don't care about your overall financial health. Their number one priority is making as much profit as possible without breaking the law. And, their shareholders expect nothing less.

Who is looking out for your best interests? YOU and YOU alone. It is one thing to let your guard down and significantly overspend on a pair of sneakers, quite another to do so with regard to housing. If your entire take home pay is regularly diverted to housing related expenses, there will be nothing left for your savings account. And, zero savings delays the accumulation of wealth and financial independence. So pick a reasonable amount to borrow under a 30 or 15 year fixed rate, no frills mortgage, after consulting your current Personal Income Statement, and you will be glad you did. Relying on someone else's formulas or "magic tricks" will harm your cash flow for years to come as they don't take *all* your expenses, liabilities, obligations and goals into consideration.

## Not Viewing Your Home as an Investment:
Some folks believe in putting all their eggs in one basket and stretching to buy the largest, most expensive house they can afford in the nicest of neighborhoods. This approach worked well in the United States for 5 plus decades (right after World War II) when jobs were plentiful and our economy was firing on all cylinders. Times are different now. Don't overreach to buy a home in the hope it will significantly increase in value. A home is not a true investment. Your housing structure (unlike the land) depreciates like a car and unless you spend considerable money updating it (new roof, driveway, bathrooms, etc.) it could be worth less than you initially paid for it.

And, bigger/more expensive means higher costs associated with utilities, property taxes and repairs. Contractors and other service people tend to charge more money to work on or in nicer homes/neighborhoods despite what their official policy may state. It's only human nature to maximize returns **when you can.** Consumers with more expensive homes can more easily afford paying a few extra dollars to fix a toilet, sink or appliance.

To revisit why primary homes are liabilities and not investments, consult Chapter 3, Section E., False Investments (Fool's Gold).

## Not Caring What Others Think:
Avoid being materialistic and adopting a "keeping up with the Joneses" approach to living. If your neighbors made recent improvements to their homes, like adding an in-ground pool, building a fancy portico or installing an elaborate play-set for their kids, resist the temptation to follow suit because you don't want to feel left out or looked down upon. Everyone's circumstances and priorities are different and you will earn the respect of others (and yourself) if you don't keep up for the right reasons. People tend to fixate more on their own situations, limitations and frailties, rather than those of others.

Do what's best for you when making personal financial decisions. (Again, don't do something simply to fit in better.) If you can't afford a pool or don't think it adds value, why not join a nearby swim club instead at a fraction of the cost and reap the additional social benefits of doing so? (An in-ground pool might cost 50k to install. If that same amount were invested and left untouched for 20 years, it could very well grow into a million dollars or more. What will the pool be worth after the same duration?) Similarly, why not enjoy the free swing/play set at your nearby park or school instead of spending 3-5k on a fancy new one for your property? Public playgrounds tend to have more bells and whistles than smaller private ones without the upkeep or liability on your part.

Too often we are like lemmings, following the actions of others without questioning "Why?" Often the why is to boost our self-esteem, gain prestige, or simply fit in due to our own insecurities. *Be an independent thinker and don't let the decisions of others compel you to act a certain way.* Your home should be a comfortable place to live and raise your family, not a place to impress others.

A bigger home with "bigger toys" will not make you any happier once its novelty wears off. And, it can hinder your ability to save enough money to become financially independent at any age. Bigger homes cost more money to maintain (i.e., heat, cool, insure and re-paint) and furnish eating into your savings rate. With a positive self-image and healthy mental outlook you can avoid "The Fatal Blow" of materialism, including coveting thy neighbor's possessions.

## D. 3 Essentials to Look For in a Home

Forget about a prospective home's exterior color, curb appeal or architectural style and focus instead on location, overall condition, and fair market value. The first three characteristics can be modified fairly easily and inexpensively, while the latter three are more permanent in nature and or can't be rectified without great additional expense. Therefore, pay particular attention when purchasing a home that it possesses *all* three of the below essentials: (It's not all about location, location, location – If you want to best position yourself for Early Financial Independence.)

**1) Great Location:** From a macro and micro standpoint. If you buy a home in a top tier/quality town (macro) in a desirable section/neighborhood within that town (micro) - you will reap three main benefits. 1) Your home will retain more of its value during an economic downturn in comparison to a similar home located in a less desirable community. 2) If your home is reasonably priced, it will be easier to sell in a shorter period of time should you need to relocate for work, raise extra cash in the event of an emergency or downsize during retirement. And, 3) There is less of a reason to send your kid(s) to private school as the public system, which you pay for through property taxes, is more than adequate to prepare them for college.

Top tier towns are readily identified by their well-publicized public school rankings. The higher the school system ranks amongst other towns/municipalities in the state (over 500 in NJ), the more desirable it is in general to live there. When it comes to locating the best sections of town, consult with long term residents, reputable real estate agents and your trusted instincts. But it does not end there. Once you identify the ideal neighborhood(s), make sure your prospective home is nestled in the heart of the neighborhood and well positioned on its lot.

Homes that are on the fringe (1st home in the section, but on a busy street or adjoining anything retail/public in nature) or built too close to the street or a neighbor's property line - negatively impact privacy, result in extra noise invading living spaces and prohibit future expansion due to zoning restrictions. Additionally, homes "shoe-horned" into tight spaces (its footprint takes up too much of the lot size) should be avoided as well as structures located in or near a flood zone or those not allowing for proper water drainage.

Why pay extra to insure your home with a separate flood insurance rider/policy, unless you have a nice view of a river, lake or ocean? Why incur the added cost and inconvenience of inheriting a shared driveway or one that can't be re-pitched to the street or backyard? (I.e., if rain water run-off is in jeopardy of entering your garage or living spaces if a sump pump fails or losses its source of electricity.) If you can think of these angles, so can other buyers.

Resist the temptation to buy the most impressive (usually biggest and most expensive) home on your street. If you can afford to do so, consider selecting a nicer section of town or more desirable community altogether. You don't want to be the big fish in a small pond when it comes to housing. You will stick out like a sore thumb, and may lose money when it comes time to sell.

**2) Solid "Bones":** Whether you purchase a split style, ranch or colonial home, be sure its backbone/major structural components (foundation, frame; roof) are in good to excellent condition. If the prospective home has decent "bones", you will significantly decrease the possibility of unexpected major expenditures in the future. And, you will be able to more easily re-sell it down the road to discriminating buyers, who are usually less price conscious.

Cosmetic fixes are fine if you buy a fixer upper at the right price. Structural repairs are quite another thing as no one wants to buy damaged goods. Unlike a broken electronic gadget that can be quickly and relatively inexpensively exchanged for an undamaged one, a home is all yours after the closing. There is no easy way to exchange it for another one. Therefore, do your best to avoid inheriting a previous owner's major problems/headaches.

With the help of an unbiased, skilled inspector, look for anything presenting challenges beyond the norm such as: Water and termite damage, the presence of radon gas and structural deficiencies in the foundation, frame or roof. Large foundation cracks, unusual settling and unstable walls or floors are all indications you should pass. Although inspectors don't always catch everything, some may intentionally overlook flaws because they are working for your realtor (live off their referrals) to aid in a quick sale. [Make no mistake about it - Your real estate agent's primary goal is to sell homes and collect commission checks. They secondarily care you are satisfied in the end with the purchase to preserve their reputation and enhance referrals, but this takes a back seat to their immediate financial gain.] Therefore, it is critical you hire an impartial third party to inspect homes, preferably from outside of the area or community you are buying in.

Hone your "street smarts" and listen to your intuition (gut feeling/instinct) as it is often more accurate than intellectual/logical reasoning, which can get clouded with emotions. One of my Professors was famous for saying – "if it quacks like a duck, waddles like a duck and smells like a duck, then it's a duck!" If a home smells musty, shows signs of past water damage, appears to have new paint on the basement and garage floors potentially concealing something – Proceed with caution and trust your gut, not your head or heart. Why would someone freshly paint their garage or basement unless it was absolutely necessary? How many other things could they have done to better stage their house and make it shine even more?

If the home is not located in a flood zone – Does its basement contain a sump pump or exhibit signs of a covered pit? If so, this may be an indication of a water problem or high water table possibly eroding the foundation. Consult neighbors about either situation, but don't always trust their feedback. They may not want to disclose problems that may make it more difficult for them to sell their own homes in the future. It is best to go down the street a bit asking for input as their allegiances may not run quite as high with the sellers (due to infrequent contact) and they may not be experiencing the same issues. You might want to start the conversation off with (after introducing yourself first) – "How long have you lived in this neighborhood?" "Do you ever recall seeing rolled up carpeting, furniture or appliances on the premises after a storm?" You might be surprised how perceptive people are about the misfortune of others.

If you have to pick between two identical homes, one with a sump pump, the other without (because it does not need one) – Go for the latter. Even if a sump pump is only activated a few times a year, the loss of electricity is often associated with storms producing heavy winds/rain and downed electrical wires. Without a backup power supply, water will enter your home (sump pump or no sump pump) damaging items in its path. Insurance may cover your losses, but, you still have to outlay a deductible, clean-up properly to avoid mold and mildew problems and replace/repair damaged items ... all at a considerable personal time expense.

**3) Good/Fair Price:** Purchasing a home will likely be the largest expenditure you ever make. Shop around and get to know the market before committing to price. A small upfront savings enables you to "bank" a sizable amount of money for funding much needed future updates or makeover projects. A 10% discount, for instance, to close quickly on a half-a-million dollar property translates into an extra $50,000 in your pocket.

Although there are many differences between stocks and real estate, one mantra applies equally to both – "Buy low, sell high" ... preferably after a long term hold to lock in additional savings. Oftentimes the biggest real estate gains are made at the time of acquisition by negotiating the *right price*, not on future appreciation.

Notice I didn't say "great price". If your prospective home is in a great location and has solid bones (meets 1st two conditions), despite needing some cosmetic fixes, odds are you will have to pay close to fair market value to land it. Nonetheless, you can often receive a small discount as a strong buyer and even beat out higher bids if you: 1) Can afford a large down payment (somewhere in the 20 to 50% range) making it less likely you will back out of the deal because of not receiving final mortgage approval. 2) Have already been pre-approved for a larger amount than you need to borrow; 3) Do not have another home to sell (1st time buyer) or the purchase of your new home is not contingent on the sale of your existing home.

It's worth mentioning - A home's list price does not always equal fair market value. Some sellers strategically start out with an artificially high sales price to allow room for future negotiation and or to factor into the equation the blood, sweat, toil and positive emotions they invested and are leaving behind in their property. Don't place too much emphasis on a seller's initial offer before counter offering. Instead, study comps (comparable homes in the same neighborhood that recently sold or are pending) and use them as your basis for computing fair value. Partner with a talented real estate agent to assist in this process. They often have knowledge (or can obtain it from other realtors) of the specific condition of the comps in question so you can better state you case for a reasonable discount. Wouldn't it be nice to know three of the four comps you are analyzing had more extensive and costly interior updates than yours and still sold for less?

Don't pay a substantial premium for a home (like paying over list price) in the hope it will not matter much years down the road when you sell. Overpaying stays with you for a long time and either diminishes your potential upside or widens/accentuates your loss. Look the other way on small purchases so you can channel your energies where it matters most – saving on big ticket items like a home.

If all three of the above housing essentials match, **great location**, **solid bones** and **good/fair price**, seriously consider buying it. A carefully selected home is capable of producing many years of happiness, priceless memories and peace of mind. And, although your home may not make you money in the end - A sound choice will put you on the fast track to achieving Early Financial Independence.

## E. Starter Homes

Don't buy an incompatible "starter home" just to get in the game. It is costly to buy and sell real estate from a closing cost (attorney fees, commissions and transfer taxes), moving expenses and re-modeling outlays perspective. And, the flaws or drawbacks you identify in a home prior to making an offer, may very well scare away prospective buyers when it comes time to sell … especially if the housing market is in an unhealthy state then.

Why purchase a home likely to be negatively impacted by a reduced pool of buyers? During difficult times, buyers tend to more closely scrutinize their purchases to conserve on dollars. And, fewer interested buyers usually means less demand and a diminished re-sale value. Think twice about buying a two bedroom home or one with three or four bedrooms if one of them is "captive". (One of the bedrooms requires you to walk through another bedroom to gain access to it, causing privacy concerns.)

Aside from cost implications, your happiness is paramount. Pick a home you can live in for years to come that will **enhance** your quality of life. If you don't really like it (or its potential), don't buy it!! (By the way, don't tell your agent you love it or have to have it. If the other side finds out, you might end up paying more for the house. Think poker face.) A house is not an investment you can count on flipping or upgrading every few years. As stated earlier - Homes are not guaranteed to increase in value and are highly illiquid (hard to convert to cash to lock in gains in a short time frame).

Additionally, moving frequently is emotionally and physically taxing. Asking your children to adjust to a new school, potentially mid-year, is stressful … As is breaking the special bonds your family has formed with neighbors, friends and certain cherished characteristics of your former surroundings. Select a home you can live in for a long time and you'll be glad you did. One of the world's richest people and most widely respected stock market investors ever, Warren Buffet, took this approach and remained in his primary home 5 plus decades after hitting it big. (Wikipedia.org, 2013)

In sum, avoid starter homes and instead opt for a more expensive entry point that will accommodate future growth and provide you with greater satisfaction. If you can't afford a home now meeting both current and future needs, don't buy. Sit back, save and be patient.

## F. Fixer-Uppers

Buying a fixer upper does not guarantee a good deal if you: 1) Are not handy. It is very expensive to hire out most projects. (It can cost as much as several hundred dollars to have a contractor prep and paint one room); 2) grossly miscalculate the cost of performing necessary upgrades. If comparable homes in good condition in the area can fetch around $500,000 and yours seems like a bargain at $450,000 ask yourself – What will it cost to bring it up to par?

I passed on two desirably located homes in 2006 that had been neglected for decades (must have had 50 year old kitchens and bathrooms with little if any updates elsewhere), because the discounting was not in line with what needed to be replaced. Redoing an entire kitchen in my neighborhood at that time cost around **20K**, while bathrooms somewhere in the **8 to 10K** range. Additionally, having to install maintenance free siding (strongly recommended over painting, because it lasts longer, is easier to maintain and less expensive if you intend to stay in your house 8 plus years), a new roof (assuming no rot on the underlying plywood) and landscaping would have conservatively tacked on another **$9k, $5K** and **3K** respectively.

Would you pay an extra 55k for the above referenced house (for a total of $505,000) if the seller did all of the aforementioned updates on your behalf to 100% of your liking? Perhaps not. The previously mentioned big ticket updates don't factor into the equation the cost of repairing or upgrading the heating/cooling/electrical systems, driveway/walkways, fixtures, plumbing, windows, doors, locks, etc. (Learn to evaluate all angles during your "to buy" or "not buy" analysis.) Although another 35K (total of 90k in outlays) might put the house in mint condition – Could you realistically get $540,000 for the home with a complete make-over? If the answer is "No" – You should pass. Even if you get to enjoy all the new updates for years to come (huge benefit of fixing up an older discounted home) – there is such a thing as overkill or reaching the point of diminishing returns.

## G. Conflicting Role of Real Estate Agents

As a buyer, you have nothing to lose by asking the seller if they will accept a lower price to get the ball rolling. It softens the beaches for your reasonably low offer and allows both real estate agents to lobby on your behalf. And they will, unless there are concurrent offers on the table or a friend/family member also wants the place. Most agents are highly motivated to collect a commission and sell as many houses as possible.

This works to your advantage. It is in the best interest of both agents to convince the seller to accept your reduced price *now*, rather than waiting for a slightly higher offer and corresponding commission check that may never arrive. A bird in the hand is worth more than two in the bush, as listings expire and people change agents. If your agent gets 1.5% when you purchase a home and the listing agent (representing the seller) gets another 1.5% - Do you think they care much if the seller gets a reduced price of 450K versus 500K (full list)? Probably not, as their commission is reduced by just $750 at the lower price point. ($7500 minus $6750)

Even though the seller stands to take the biggest hit at a 50K reduction in price, and neither agent would likely accept the reduced offer if it were their own home, the agents will probably encourage the sale. ("The illusion of purity hides corruption", Freakonomics) When the seller's agent recommends their client accept your low but "reasonable" offer – What they may really be saying is it does not benefit me, the agent, to hold out any longer, so let's take the money and run. (Plaintiff's lawyers do the same thing when settling Personal Injury cases.)

## H. Basements – A "Near Essential" in Some Places

Don't purchase a home in certain regions unless it has a basement. (Shore/vacation homes not included.) Basements make homes in the Northeast, for example, more temperate from a climate control standpoint. They do so by providing "extra separation"/insulation between the main living quarters (typically the first and/or second floors) and the raw, damp earth.

When homes are built on a slab (a piece of thick concrete directly touching the ground at a point above the frost line) or over a crawl space (an un-usable ½ basement of sorts that can't be heated or cooled effectively), they tend to introduce extra dampness and cold into your living space. This, in turn, requires the use of more heat to off-set or neutralize, such as ambient/in-floor heating coils installed in or over the slab.

Additional benefits of having a basement:

- They are a great place to store items. This extra storage comes in handy when you have kids and allows you to free up garage space so you can actually park a car or two in there during inclement weather.
- You can convert a portion of it into an extra "living" room complete with exercise equipment, a couch and television.
- It is a nice place to conceal your furnace, hot water heater and laundry machines (washer/dryer) from a noise reduction standpoint. And should they ever leak, excess water can be easily diverted to a French drain or sump pump pit.

On the downside, basements are a liability because an electric sump pump installation is often required. A sump pump prevents excess ground water (beneath the basement floor) from entering the room, usually after storms or when transitioning from winter to spring ... when the ground is thawing and melting ice/snow travels from the surface to the underground temporarily raising the water table. And, if you lose power during a storm, without a battery backup system or generator - Your basement could become flooded, potentially damaging everything in it, including your expensive furnace. (Tip: Always put your furnace on blocks.)

Additionally, almost every basement requires a dehumidifier, which removes excess humidity/moisture from the air and prevents mold and mildew from accumulating in the area. Some homes without basements (i.e. on slabs) still need a dehumidifier, but their units don't tend to run as often as those located in basements. The more the dehumidifier operates - The more electricity it requires and the more often you will need to replace it with a new one. (They typically last 3- 5 years on average.)

Having owned a home with and without a basement – I couldn't easily do without one now and consider them a **necessary luxury** regardless of their added cost.

## I. Importance of Attractive Landscaping

A well-manicured lawn with attractive landscaping increases the value of a home and makes it easier to sell. When prospective buyers are impressed with a home's exterior from the street/curb, they often want to see more. And, their positive first impressions of the outside can produce a "halo effect" that carries over into their evaluation of the interior design and layout.

If you can "wow" prospective buyers with an inviting exterior (including landscaping) and a clutter free, well maintained interior, you should be able to get a higher percentage of them to reward you with bona fide offers. The more interested buyers, the more likely you will receive concurrent offers increasing the chances of getting top dollar for your home.

Although the condition of a home's roof, shingles/siding, windows, front door, etc. play a major role in shaping positive first impressions, quality landscaping is as important. The addition of decorative trees, bushes and plants, set in well-trimmed mulch or rock-lined beds, adds a nice finishing touch, sure to impress. Since the benefits of a favorable first impression linger on well beyond a buyer's initial house tour – Why not put your best foot forward? What do you have to lose?

Additional considerations on using landscaping to your monetary advantage:

- Consider purchasing a home with poor "curb appeal" if the home is discounted enough. It is fairly easy and relatively inexpensive to replace overgrown bushes with more attractive varieties. And, an un-kept exterior may frighten away some buyers, making it more likely the seller will accept your discounted offer. (Sellers whose homes have been on the market a while, tend to be more flexible in their pricing negotiations.)
- With regard to professional landscapers, don't be shocked by their high prices! The more items they plant, the more money they make for themselves and their affiliated nurseries/garden centers. Why not duplicate or modify one of their proposed layouts if you are impressed with it? You can easily save a thousand or more dollars by digging your own holes and spreading your own mulch, something that doesn't require much skill to accomplish successfully. As an added bonus, you will be able to bask in the glow of a job well done every time you pull into your driveway.
- Buying in bulk makes perfect sense for fill dirt, top-soil and mulch. You'll receive a discount for purchasing large quantities and may qualify for free delivery, if you are able to commit to "x" yards, eliminating the hassle of having to make many time consuming trips back and forth to your local supply store. (A yard is essentially a large bulldozer scoop.) When establishing new mulch beds adjoining your house - You may require plenty of fill dirt to aide

in raising and re-grading the area so rain water run-off is naturally diverted away from your home's foundation.
- Don't over landscape. Too many mulch beds, shrubs and gardens mean extra maintenance and added expense ... from additional pruning, feeding, watering, weeding, mulching and edging. Likewise, too many plantings packed into a condensed area might look good in the beginning when the plants are small. But, when they start to grow - you may need to transplant some elsewhere to prevent over-crowding and damage. Be sure to research the average maturation dimensions (width and height) of your plantings and space accordingly.
- A classic or traditional landscape design is optimal. It has staying power and will appeal to a larger pool of buyers. Adorning your yard with exotic stands of bamboo, pink flamingos and boxwoods carved into animal shapes will do more harm than good from a curb appeal standpoint and may infuriate your neighbors. Both losing propositions.
- Invest in yard and garden equipment when first starting out in a home. You will save considerable money mowing your grass and performing other necessary outdoor tasks, instead of outsourcing these. And, at a critical time when your savings account can use the extra padding. You can usually find used, reasonably priced lawnmowers, wheel barrows, trimmers, rakes and other items at garage/house sales. As an added benefit of doing your own: You will appreciate all the more someday being able to you hire a landscaper should your finances improve, freeing up valuable time to attend to your career and children.
- Be vigilant about eradicating weeds. When weeds take hold of your lawn, they "squeeze out" desirable grass, eventually killing and further enabling additional unsightly weeds to grow. It's much easier and more cost effective controlling or reducing weed growth (can't eliminate it all together) than planting and nurturing new grass from seed. When you re-seed sections of your lawn, it must be watered twice a day for weeks on end (depending on weather conditions) so the young grass can establish deep roots and thrive. It takes a lot of water to do so and you can expect your water bill to double as a result.
- Have work done in the off season. For instance, pruning or removing trees in the winter months. Reputable tree care experts experience a lull in business during this time and are willing to offer compelling discounts to keep their employees, contractors and or friends gainfully employed. The winter is an ideal season for having whole trees removed. The ground is usually frozen (reducing damage to your lawn from heavy equipment and falling debris) and there is zero risk dead branches will be overlooked since the entire tree is being taken down.

## J. Saving on Furnishings

Home furnishings, like couches, tables and chairs are expensive, especially ones built to last. Therefore, when getting established in your first home, don't rush to fill it in the name of comfort and convenience. If you don't take sufficient time searching for good deals, you will overpay for what you buy.

Home furnishings are not necessities like food or clothes. You can make do without them for a while (several years if need be) and improvise where it makes sense ... Such as using an inexpensive folding table in the dining room with outdoor plastic stacking chairs to entertain on infrequent holidays.

Your patience will be rewarded with significant savings if you:

- *Buy used furniture.* You can find pieces in excellent condition at private home and estate sales at a fraction of the price of new ones. I purchased a dining room set, after months of scouring local classified ads, for several thousand dollars less than retail from someone who was downsizing.
- *Shop at discount warehouses and going out-of-business sales.* These venues are great for items you may not feel comfortable buying in used condition, like couches or mattresses. Some stores institute a same day cash and carry policy and you may need to transport your purchases back home in a rented van. The significant price savings is well worth the hassle.
- *Frequent garage sales and thrift shops for lower-end items.* Lamps, mirrors, picture frames, paintings and end tables, to name a few, can all be had for rock bottom prices at garage sales and thrift shops. Many people, especially those in nicer homes and neighborhoods, collect far more "stuff" than they need. Rather than tossing the items to the curb (throw away), they often attempt to sell them on their own or donate them to charitable organizations – Many of which operate thrift stores to convert goods to much needed cash. Tip: Don't steer clear of slightly damaged items. Scratches and other imperfections can usually be concealed or filled so they are much less noticeable.
- *Decorate using high quality traditional furnishings.* That way you don't need to update/replace them any more frequently than you want to. Traditional or classic furnishings stand the test of time by not looking dated or out of style after only a few years of use. When in doubt, select solid neutral colors or simple designs over loud, complex, trendy ones. Conservative, but elegant handmade wool area rugs, for instance, should last a lifetime and can be rolled up and brought with you wherever you decide to live next.
- *Apply the applicable "7 Ways to Save" principles (outlined in Chapter 4).* Comparison shopping, for instance, is the only way to go for big ticket items. It pays to

shop around, negotiate for improved discounts and use cash whenever possible to maximize what you get to keep in your pocket ... even if it takes substantial time to do so.

## K. Reap Additional Savings on Housing-Related Expenses by:

- Considering buying a two family "starter" home. The income generated from renting one side, floor or unit can substantially offset the costs associated with your primary living space ... Making this a less expensive option than buying a single family home.
- Maintaining an excellent credit rating so your borrowing costs (interest on your mortgage) are as low as possible and you are not forced into paying additional upfront loan fees, such as points (pre-paying interest). Higher risk borrowers, such as those with maxed out credit cards or a pattern of not paying their bills on time - spend more to obtain financing than lower risk borrowers. With the former, there is a greater likelihood the loan will not be repaid in full (go into foreclosure), hence the price difference to compensate the lender for additional risk.
- Researching potential solutions to home repair issues *before* committing to contractors. If you can "talk shop" with a contractor, you are less likely to be taken advantage of. Obtaining three price quotes (highly recommended for major projects) is an educational process in its own right and will shed additional light on your options, especially if you ask good questions.
- Buying upfront yourself quality materials, repair parts and or finished goods for a job so you only need to compare hourly labor rates.
- Developing close relationships with local suppliers and receiving discounts and other perks in exchange for your *loyalty*. Loyalty is best expressed by shopping somewhere regularly over the long term without "nickel-and-diming" them. When suppliers know they can count on your business through thick and thin -You will be rewarded.
- Sharing expensive or seldom used equipment and tools with friends and neighbors. However, this may be more trouble than it's worth if you are not highly selective. Others may not take good care of what you co-purchase and share, resulting in added repair and replacement costs.
- Being nice to those you employ in and around your home. Showing them the same level of respect you yourself would want to receive, regardless of job title or socio-economic background. The quality of their work might just be related to how well you treat them. When appropriate, supply free beverages,

snacks and meals as a show of appreciation. Money is not the only powerful motivator of human behavior. If you treat someone fairly, they will usually return the favor.

- If garbage or waste removal services are not included in your town's property tax bill, shop around for a low cost provider. You may have the ability to select your own trash hauler from a long list of names and bigger isn't always better when it comes to service and price. When obtaining quotes, ask if you are entitled to a discount if you pay "x" months in advance.

- Using the same insurance company for multiple products (home, car; "umbrella"). You must insure your home and car to satisfy lender requirements and or state mandates. Why not cover both through the same entity if you are entitled to an additional discount for doing so? And, when your net worth reaches a certain value, consider purchasing a Personal Catastrophe Liability (aka "umbrella") policy. Such a policy protects your assets from being sold to satisfy personal judgments against you. (Personal judgments are awarded to people/plaintiffs who successfully sue you in court for injuries/damages you as a defendant negligently caused.)

- Refinancing your mortgage if interest rates drop enough. This can result in substantial savings *after* a break even period. Whether a one or two percent interest rate reduction is enough to act on depends upon how you answer: How much longer do you realistically intend to live in your home? Is there enough time remaining on your current loan to make it worthwhile? And, what out of pocket costs must you incur now to realize future savings? Note: It may make more sense to switch to a 15 year loan when refinancing instead of starting all over again with another 30 year obligation period.

- Purchasing a home you can afford on one salary or a small portion of a second one. There may come a time when you or your spouse is voluntarily or involuntarily "separated" from the workforce. Taking care of young children, tending to a serious personal illness or dealing with long term unemployment may put a temporary halt to an otherwise lucrative career. If you purchase a home requiring two full time incomes to support, the loss of one income stream for a prolonged period of time can spell DISASTER. Not being able to make your monthly mortgage payments leads to foreclosure or having to unload your home in a hurry at less than an optimal price.

- Appealing your property tax assessment should the numbers work to your advantage. Aside from your monthly mortgage payment, property taxes are the next largest on-going expenditure associated with your home. Since they can never be paid off and rarely decrease, major thought should be given to their long term affordability *before* buying a home. And, even if you can afford

- the property taxes, consider filing for a re-assessment with your local tax collector for a permanent reduction. But, do your homework first. You may end up paying more if you lose the appeal, especially if you have recently completed major home improvements.
- Downsizing if you buy too much home. Getting in over your head with real estate is far from ideal. There is a surcharge or premium of sorts associated with doing so in the form of higher monthly mortgage payments, taxes, utilities and maintenance costs. We all make mistakes. If you learn from them, you can turn things around and strengthen your long term position. As long as you are not in denial and recognize you are on an unsustainable course (half the battle), you can reverse your misfortune by selling your too costly of a home and purchasing a more affordable one so you can live below your means.
- Avoiding homes that are adjacent to public property or private recreational areas. Purchasing a home backing up to a park, golf course or nature preserve might seem appealing at first. However, what if the land changes hands, is re-purposed or re-zoned and the golf course you fell in love with is converted to a residential apartment complex? Instead of an occasional golf ball in your backyard, you could end up with a frequent supply of annoying litter, debris and noise/light pollution from the adjoining development. The net financial impact of the land conversion to you: A decreased home value.
- Using coarse sand over salt (or the imitation stuff) for icy sidewalks, steps and driveways. Sand, when liberally applied, provides enough traction on slippery surfaces to reduce the risk of injures from falls. It is also less expensive than salt and does not deteriorate or corrode concrete, limestone, asphalt or pavers. This latter benefit alone has significant positive cost implications and is enough of a reason to flex to its use beyond being more environmentally friendly.

In summary, some form of housing is a necessity. However, miscalculating the total cost of ownership component and how it impacts your unique "Personal Income Statement" can destabilize your financial situation for a very long time. Don't let new-found independence get the best of you by overspending on housing, even if it meets the three essentials (great location, solid bones and a good/fair price). And, make sure you can afford all aspects of renting or owning, not just for today and tomorrow, *but for the long haul.* **Living below your means** is the best way to go, whether you purchase a compatible starter home or economically attractive fixer upper with poor curb appeal. Adhering to this key principle will enable you to smartly furnish your home inside and out and succeed at focusing on and winning in the other major sections of this guide.

# CHAPTER 6

## Transportation

*Purchasing an expensive motor vehicle is almost always non-advisable if you want to attain Early Financial Independence (EFI).*

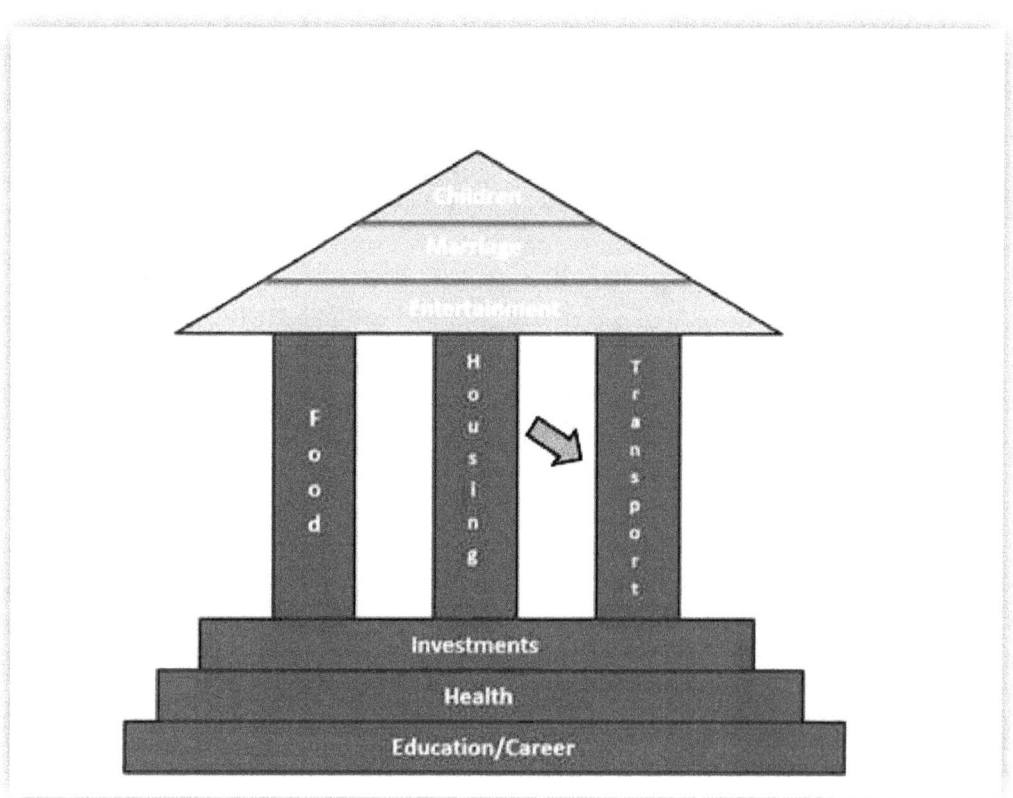

Building & maintaining EFI by managing your "spend"/focus on transportation.

Unless a true collectible, cars, trucks and everything in between are assets (*not* investments) that depreciate substantially over time until their eventual worth is "junk value". The weather (sun, rain and wind), environment (humidity, salt and road conditions), general wear and tear through repeated use (i.e., high mileage) and increased age "eats" at cars until their parts rust, decompose or otherwise break down.

Any new/used car (a term used interchangeably with "vehicle") you buy, no matter how shiny, sleek and fast, will steadily lose value until it's only worth its weight in recycled materials and or the sum total of its salvageable replacement parts. Although you can **delay** the inevitable by rebuilding your car at every turn, you will reach a point where it is no longer practical to do so from a pure dollars and cents standpoint. Does spending $1000 to repair a 15 year old car with a value of $1500 make sense? Shouldn't you instead apply the repair costs to a newer vehicle since an even greater fix may be lurking around the corner?

## A. Transportation's Relevance to Savings Guide?

Plain and simple - Failure to keep your transportation costs in check will negatively impact **in a disproportionate manner** your ability to save enough cash to attain EFI.

Getting from Point A to Point B is a costly proposition. Unless you rely exclusively on public bus or rail service, which is somewhat affordable because it is commonly subsidized with taxpayer dollars - transportation related expenses, including owning a car, will likely take the third largest bite out of your personal budget …right behind housing and college loan repayment obligations.

Therefore, it pays to keep tight control over your transportation spend, whether it be for work related matters, running household errands or going for leisurely rides by adhering to three key transportation saving practices: (Foregoing car ownership as long as practical, not overspending on a vehicle; staying focused on obtaining price concessions.)

### 1) Forgoing Car Ownership as Long as Practical

For an affordable start in life- when you are in high school and college, walk, bike or take public transportation whenever you can. Owning a car is very costly and the longer you forgo ownership, the more money you will be able to save and or divert to more important uses, such as obtaining a quality education.

When you want to explore off campus destinations, borrow your parent's car or rent one for the day/week. Why own something as expensive and infrequently needed as a car in your early years until you absolutely can't live without one? (Like when you land a job that requires you to get to the office or meet with clients.) Shouldn't your car earn its keep, especially when you have little excess to spend on luxuries? (Note:

Most rental car companies will only rent to more "experienced" drivers, those defined as 21 or older.)

To cope without a car - Buy a good bike and excellent walking/running shoes for short trips to compliment public transportation, like on-campus shuttles. And, because the price of fuel will likely remain relatively high over time, live within walking distance to where you need to be on a regular basis, such as academic buildings, dining halls, train stations and internship/residency programs. Some folks predict living in the suburbs or on the fringes of towns will become an even more expensive proposition someday. I believe they are right.

## 2) Not Overspending on a Vehicle

When shopping for a car finally makes sense, resist the temptation to spend too much. Owning *any* car is a luxury and liability rolled up into one that comes with major responsibilities.

**Form of Luxury** - Car ownership is a luxury, not a necessity/essential like food and water. You can survive quite well without a car and there are suitable alternatives should you plan accordingly. And, driving a car on public roads is not even a protected legal right. It is a privilege highly regulated by State law. Without a valid driver's license, proper registration and insurance, your car can't leave your driveway.

You may counter: How can a car be a luxury if everyone seems to have one, especially during rush hour when there appears to be an endless supply on the road? Appearances can be deceiving. How many bus stops or train stations did you pass during the same commute where countless folks were traveling without a car, many by forced circumstances? Or, how many residences did you drive by where the inhabitants were unable to make it to a public transportation source due to financial constraints?

Having access to some form of transportation is essential. If you can't move easily between places, you will be unable to obtain a quality education or land a meaningful job. Avoiding the entitlement mindset (others have cars, so should I) will go a long way in separating you from the pack and making you financially free *before* your 40's … An accomplishment worth the sacrifice.

**Quasi Liability** – From a pure accounting standpoint, a car is an asset unless you owe more on it than what you could sell it for. Cars contribute to your net worth (Net worth = assets minus liabilities), since they can be sold for cash (another form of asset) that can be used to directly reduce your debt/liability.

As exciting as this classification may seem, most financially successful people view their cars as a liability, even if purchased outright with zero debt. 1) Cars don't create income resulting in relatively high **opportunity costs.** (More on opportunity costs later.) 2) They constantly lose value to depreciation, even on day 1 when first driven off a dealer's lot, gradually diminishing your net worth in the process. And, 3) They generate on-going expenses, including but not limited to, routine and not so routine maintenance/repair costs, loan/interest payments and mandatory operational costs such as liability insurance, fuel and parking fees.

Although some cars hold their value better than others, this does not mean they are a true investment or even a good buy. Ask yourself – Is the upfront premium paid to obtain a higher re-sale value vehicle worth it (from a pure financial perspective) when it comes time to trade it in for another one? "No" is the answer most of the time as it costs more to service, replace parts, and insure higher end vehicles for theft and collision. In contrast, working professionals needing to make a "statement of success" to retain and attract additional clients/patients/customers usually answer "yes". (This is typically the case for real estate agents and other sales professionals.) Even more so when they own a business (like lawyers and medical doctors) and can expense a premium vehicle as an operating cost, much like advertising and promotional programs.

### 3) Staying Focused to Obtain Price Concessions

Channel your precious time and energy into obtaining sizable discounts on big ticket transportation purchases, like cars, car insurance premiums and major repairs, where the savings return can be significant. And, if and only if there is enough time left over, should you devote it to obtaining bargains on miscellaneous lesser purchases - not the other way around.

Earning a 20% reduction in yearly transportation costs, a realistic goal, could easily net you $1000 or more in savings with a ten hour time investment. (Return of $100 per hour.) By contrast, the same reduction related to your yearly footwear consumption may only put an extra $100 in your pocket after several hours of comparison shopping. (Return of around $14.00 per hour.) Which endeavor should you focus on first? Getting lost in the details without seeing the big picture costs money. Strategically prioritizing your time shopping for discounts will prevent this from happening!

## B. What Type of Vehicle Should You Purchase to Keep Costs in Check?

Short answer: Any reasonably priced ride that will safely and reliably get you from one destination to the next. (You don't have to spend a fortune on a vehicle to obtain quality, nor should you buy the cheapest car on the lot simply because it is the least expensive option.) As stated earlier, all motor vehicles depreciate and lose value over time as they are simply not investments. The more you spend on one, the more you lose. Even quality luxury sedans, which hold their value better than lesser made makes and models, are worth less over time.

Before purchasing a vehicle meeting your needs, be sure to consult expert reviews. Consumer Reports publishes an excellent yearly guide to selecting automobiles based on several scoring/consideration factors. If you are single and don't need a lot of interior space, a smaller more fuel efficient vehicle may do the trick. Most guides classify "best buy" purchase recommendations by class (i.e., compact, mid-size; large) and price range.

## C. The Importance of "Living Below" Your Transportation Means

The more you spend on a car, beyond a certain price point, does not guarantee better performance. If you are a professional race car driver, minor differences matter. But, if you are a practical driver who values creating a nest egg, you should view cars as fun tools not status symbols. Status is something you earn rather than buy. And, if family, friends and neighbors look down on you based on your "wheels", too bad for them. They need to re-examine their priorities and become less self-absorbed.

By adopting the philosophy of "who cares what others think" you will develop thicker skin and be much better armed to cope with life's difficulties … of which there will be plenty along the way, in addition to many, many good times, I might add.

Some well-off folks prefer to drive older cars and/or more modest models. If you think about it, it makes perfect sense. People who are financially independent through their own efforts tend to live below their means in *all* areas. Transportation is no exception. They will tell you –"Don't buy as much car as you can afford. Doing so is wasteful unless it enhances your image with clients." And even then, you don't need to go overboard to prove you manage a successful career/practice. [I personally knew an accomplished surgeon who for years drove an older model station wagon to meet patients at his office, despite being able to afford so much more.] Besides, why broadcast your wealth? It only makes you a bigger target for thieves … Another reason to live modestly.

Sure it would be nice to drive a fancy sports car. But take pride in keeping your eye on the prize (EFI) and staying the course by exercising sound financial discretion. If it's any consolation – Far too many people to count in this world (perhaps a billion or more) would love to drive what you are driving. Appreciating what you have, instead of fixating on what you don't have, is a great way to stay focused on achieving important life goals.

## D. Opportunity Costs – Why They Matter

An opportunity cost is "the cost of an alternative that must be forgone in order to pursue a certain action. Put another way, the benefits you could have received by taking an alternative action." (http://www.investopedia.com)

In the world of personal transportation choices, it might translate to - What you spend on a car as a college freshman, might prevent you from taking one extra class each semester and purchasing a tablet device with all the latest educational apps. Having to forego classes and a tablet (because you don't have an infinite supply of cash for everything you want or need) is the opportunity cost of buying a car in this scenario.

But, the opportunity costs don't necessarily end there. Upon closer examination, you may discover that purchasing the car (instead of occasionally borrowing one) has negative implications years down the road, like preventing you from graduating early with one less semester of room and board to pay for. Or, conversely, graduating early, but without the use of an educational tablet device ... resulting in slightly lower grades that prevent you from attending a quality graduate school. Your choices have implications. What you don't spend on a car, you get to "invest" elsewhere.

## E. "Investing the Difference" – A Smart Move for Extra Savings

Hopefully, your first job out of college pays six figures and you can afford a luxury car. But, just because you can afford one does not mean you should buy one. There are hidden opportunity costs associated with doing so.

Purchasing a flashy $60,000 luxury vehicle, over a $25,000 comfortably equipped model, will end up costing you much more than the initial $35,000 difference. For starters, assuming an all cash purchase with zero financing, the extra 35K tied up in the luxury vehicle will deprive you of being able to use it to generate guaranteed interest come with a reputable bank or broker. The "lost"/foregone interest income could be significant if you hold onto the luxury car for many years. $35K invested for around 10 years at a constant year over year APY of 7% will double your money. (Remember the Rule of 72?) **How does having 70K in the bank sound when it comes time to replace your aging car?** That could very well be the case if you selected the lesser priced model and wisely invested the price difference.

Although the sting of lost income is lessened when you re-sell or trade-in a luxury vehicle (luxury cars tend to hold their value better than others), luxury vehicles as stated earlier cost a premium to service and insure. A simple oil change for a high-end car could easily cost more than double that of an average vehicle. Multiply that extra spend over the life of your car and you could be looking at an additional $500 to $1000 for just oil changes depending on total miles driven. This may not seem like a lot when spread out over a decade. But, small numbers have a way of adding up to big numbers.

## F. Used over New? – It's not that Simple

As a general rule, buying a gently used, well maintained car directly from a private owner is the way to go and will more often than not yield impressive savings. New and used car dealers have to markup their vehicles to cover salaries, utilities, borrowing costs, advertising fees and other expenses a private seller does not have to recoup. And, regardless of who sells you a brand new vehicle - The moment you drive it off the lot, it loses value. Why not let someone else take that one time hit for you?

Look for used cars with low miles that are ideally no more than two to three years old (that way you can keep them a while) and get them inspected by a trusted mechanic before signing on the dotted line. The last thing you want is to inherit someone else's headaches or overpay for a vehicle that needs hidden repairs. If you discover it was previously involved in a major accident or suffered flood damage – PASS!

**Exception 1A -** New cars can be better buys than used ones when car makers offer compelling year end incentives, rebates or special offers on "leftovers" to make room for newer models. To capitalize on major savings, be flexible on color, trim and other options (or lack thereof) and avoid being up-sold on costly extras, such as high-end entertainment systems, fancy rims or cool sun-roofs. Although a new car will almost always cost more than an identical used one, some price difference is justifiable. A new one has almost no miles, zero "wear and tear" and a full warranty.

**Exception 1B** – Certain new cars are better buys during recessions (tough economic times) when used car prices tend to rise on increased demand and supply reductions. Cash strapped consumers hold onto vehicles longer (don't trade them in as frequently) when money is tight. And, they mostly replace older vehicles out of necessity, shunning the higher absolute cost of new ones and gravitating towards cheaper used models, further driving up prices. As a result, *some* new car models can be had on the cheap in comparison to their over-inflated used counterparts. (Not as applicable with high end vehicles where the average consumer is less price sensitive and not as apt to suffer as much from economic downturns.) I have seen this to be particularly true with a select group of large family sedans considered "boring", "old school" or "stodgy" in design by many prospective buyers. Why pay a premium for a popular vehicle's youthful appeal or sportiness? Shouldn't safety, reliability, value and comfort be major considerations?

Whatever route you take, new or used, do your homework before making a decision. When you are ready to buy a car, or whatever it may be called by then, there may be new market factors in effect impacting the basic fundamentals of supply and demand. Use your intellect to identify future exceptions.

## G. Buy Versus Lease?

It is a matter of personal preference whether to buy or lease a vehicle as the pros and cons to each approach vary based on individual circumstances. If saving money is your main priority, buying a vehicle is the right decision *if* you plan on driving it for many years (7 plus in my informal estimation).

According to most money experts, it is ***always*** more expensive to lease a car versus own over the long haul. When you think about it – It makes perfect sense. After all, shouldn't you have to pay a premium for the prestige and convenience of being able to ride a new fully warranted car every two or three years without the hassle of having to negotiate trade-ins or private sales? (www.leaseguide.com)

In addition to the "always driving a new car cost", there are hidden extras to leasing that you would not incur if you bought. For instance, driving a leased vehicle over a certain number of contractually stipulated miles will cost you "x" amount per mile. The same applies to not servicing your leased vehicle frequently enough. If you don't return it in really good condition, there will be penalties to pay … Not true if you forget a few oil changes or get dinged in a car you own.

Aside from the added costs of leasing, when your lease period expires, you have no equity (value/worth) to show for it. Purchasing a car, on the other hand, allows you to build equity and to be payment free at some point. And, when you don't have a monthly car payment to make, you also don't have on-going borrowing costs to deal with. What is having one less financial worry worth? Better health perhaps?

If you can afford to buy a car with cash, do so! Unless you are in business for yourself and can deduct the monthly finance payment, don't borrow money to buy a car. Purchase it outright. And, if you can't afford to do so, wait until you can. The only exception should be when you are first getting started out of school … you may have no choice but to borrow money to obtain a car. Remember - Cash is king and may allow you to negotiate the lowest possible price for your vehicle.

## H. Negotiating Tips

Learning to negotiate well has broad real world applicability and will benefit you in many facets of life beyond purchasing a vehicle. Therefore, don't hesitate to take an "Art of Negotiation" class or consult a good book on the subject. The skills you will learn are invaluable.

Some negotiation techniques to use when shopping for a vehicle:

- Knowing exactly what you can afford *before* starting the process is essential. Your best negotiated price may not match the "out-the-door" price, which

contains state taxes, registration/title fees and extras such as anti-theft glass etching and dealer "document processing" fees.
- Research average selling prices ahead of time for the exact make and model you are interested in. Utilize powerful on-line apps/tools revealing what others in your zip code recently paid for the very same vehicle. Shame on you if you go into the dealer uneducated. They will then have the upper hand.
- Don't speak first when it comes to pricing. Studies have shown that he who offers up a number first loses. Let the salesperson tell you what their best price is before making a counter-offer.
- Never accept a vehicle's sticker price no matter what the retailer's published policy is. Some dealers offer a haggle free everyday low price hoping you will not ask for a better deal. There is always room for a lower price than the posted sticker amount.
- You will likely need to speak to the salesperson's boss to get the very best pricing. The reps covering the floor/lot don't usually have the authority to discount below a certain price percentage. And even if they could, they might be reluctant to do so if further reductions negatively impact their commission structure in a major way. Management and owners have a different take. They may want to move cars off their lots even if profit margins are razor slim to free up cash, receive special recognition/incentives from manufacturers and or to introduce you to their service center for profitable future repairs.
- Be polite throughout the negotiation process. Communicating a sincere "please" and "thank you" (body language/demeanor included) goes a long way in helping your cause. People assist those they like. If you act like a jerk, the sales rep may send you walking even if it means less money for them. Being respected can be as important or even more important, than being well compensated. Remember - money isn't everything from a human behavior motivation standpoint.
- Always ask for a cash discount *at the end* of the process. Although based on my car buying experience, a check has been as good as cash to sellers - it never hurts to ask for an additional cash discount. It works for many other products/services and may come into vogue again with car dealers.
- Essential last step - Even if you want the car and feel good about the price, proceed to leave the lot to get the very best deal. The dealership knows if you are a serious buyer and are willing to drive off the lot in your own vehicle, someone else may get their sale. More often than not, if there is additional price relief to be had, they will "sweeten the pot" as you head for your car.

## I. Importance of Keeping Your Car in Excellent Condition
Taking good care of your car pays dividends both emotionally and financially:

- You will **feel good** about driving your car longer (where the big returns are) if you keep it nice inside and out. If you let it become run-down, it becomes easier to look the other way on small repairs. Before you know it, you will be driving a car you can't wait to replace.
- If you keep your car well maintained (regular oil changes, new brakes, well-polished exterior; carpet protectors), it will contribute to a **higher re-sale value.** "An ounce of prevention is worth a pound of cure." (Ben Franklin) This is as applicable to cars as your own health. Failing to regularly change your engine oil, for instance, can damage your engine resulting in costly repairs. Should that ever become the case – You will wish you had paid the much cheaper oil changes along the way.

Since you will not be able to keep your car in good condition on your own, unless you are very handy, find a trusted mechanic/shop to do so. But, continue to keep them honest from time to time by getting a 2$^{nd}$ or 3$^{rd}$ price quote on expensive repairs. If you do business with primarily one shop, odds are they will treat you better because of your loyalty/repeat business. They keep detailed records on the maintenance they provide your car and will know if you are taking it elsewhere.

Avoid the temptation to chase specials regardless of who is offering them. Not all vendors are reputable and the seemingly inexpensive $15 oil change promotion at a local competitor may be a loss leader to "find" unnecessary repairs. My brother once caught a repair shop slashing a hole in a lubricating "boot" near one of his tires during a low cost oil change to generate additional business. To reiterate - Use the same trusted mechanic for almost everything. Cheap services are designed to lure you in for legitimate and illegitimate reasons and can result in unexpected costs.

Lastly, consider renting an unlimited mileage rental car for long trips when your own car is on the older side (7 plus years). Older cars tend to break down more than newer cars when pushed to the limit … Like driving them several continuous hours in the hot summer heat. And their repairs can be quite costly in relation to the price of routine maintenance services (oil, brake and tire changes). Also, the fewer miles you put on your own vehicle (within reason), the more it will be worth come trade-in or re-sale time.

## J. Saving on Car Insurance

- Before purchasing a car, research its safety rating. Cars with high crash test and roll-over scores are more likely to protect you and your passengers from sustaining serious injuries in collisions and therefore have lower overall insurance premiums than less safe models. (The National Highway Traffic Safety Administration at SaferCar.gov uses a 5 star ratings system allowing you to compare multiple makes and models.)
- Call your insurance carrier before buying a car to see what it would cost to insure for theft. Some cars are more highly prized by thieves than others and are thus more expensive to insure for that provision due to the added risk/likelihood of a pay-out.
- Be careful where you park your car, especially overnight or on the street. It is more likely to get hit, vandalized or stolen when not parked in a private driveway or safe off-the-street lot. And, the more accidents/incidents you report, regardless of whether you were in the car at the time, the higher your insurance rates will become. Your car is worth thousands of dollars and shouldn't be left anywhere. If something doesn't feel right, act on those feelings and park elsewhere.
- Shop around for car insurance – Rates can vary significantly from carrier to carrier. And, oftentimes a bundle (car, homeowners and personal liability/umbrella protection) with one company is the best way to obtain deep discounting. One word of caution, don't over-insure. During the beginning stages of your career, there is no need for an umbrella policy if you don't own a home and have little money in the bank.
- Take a defensive driving course to save 5% to 15% on your car insurance rates. This may be a necessity if you already have points on your driving record.

## K. Miscellaneous Transportation-Related Savings Tips:

- Don't make price the sole buying criteria. Purchasing the cheapest vehicle in its class will likely cost more in the long run. Research your options as less reliable, low cost vehicles usually result in more repairs than higher cost "recommended best buy" models. And, the latter tend to hold their values longer and are easier to sell on the used car market. Buyers gravitate towards make/models with a reputation for quality and durability.
- Buy a make and model car you really like. Odds are high if you settle for something "subpar" you will be selling it before the optimal 7 to 10 year retention period. What's another $1000 spread out over 10 years if it's going

to make you happy and want to keep your vehicle in decent shape for a long time?
- Keep your car for many years before getting another. It is a luxury to trade your car in every 2-4 years, regardless of whether you lease or purchase a new/newer one outright: 1) New cars are more expensive to insure than older ones. 2) To acquire them, you must withdraw money out of the bank, losing valuable interest in the process (opportunity cost). And, 3) You are on the hook again for state sales and use tax, which alone can run well over $1000 dollars on a conservative model.
- When you have a young family, safety and practicality are paramount. Trying to squeeze two kids of any age into the almost non-existent backseat of a sports car doesn't make sense. Sure, it may be super fun to drive - But what if you get into a fender bender? Will it provide as much protection as something larger with a higher safety rating?
- Don't buy a light truck for occasionally hauling large items. That is what renting or paying a store for delivery is for. Ask yourself before buying - What will your primary mode of transportation be used for the vast majority of the time? If you are a skilled tradesman, a truck is a no-brainer. If you need it to commute to work via a highway five days a week, it is not your best choice from a comfort and gas mileage standpoint.
- Don't feel compelled to own two cars when married. You and your spouse may be able to get by just fine with one reliable vehicle. If your spouse also works, this may prove more difficult, but keep an open mind to commuting together if the logistics allow, such as working near one another. According to some studies, it costs several thousand dollars a year to operate a second vehicle by the time you factor in car insurance, fuel bills, maintenance costs and depreciation. There is a good reason the IRS allows you to deduct "X" amount per mile as a legitimate business expense when using your personal car for work related matters beyond commuting to and from your main office.
- Borrow a family car rather than rent until you lose the stigma of being a young inexperienced driver. Most major rental car companies assess a sizable surcharge to renters under the age of 25 to compensate them for the added statistical risk an accident might occur. That's just the way it is. Accidents translate into personal and property damage, both of which have the potential to result in large payouts.
- Sell your used vehicle on your own. A dealer's trade-in value is *always* less than what you can obtain from a private buyer. (Middlemen receive an extra fee/cut for their service. That's why it is important to buy direct when you can, across all product lines when it makes sense.) However, trade-ins reduce the sales tax you pay on a replacement vehicle. (7% in NJ as of 2013) If you trade-in a car

worth $7K on the private market for $6K – It's really like getting $6,420 for it when you figure in the reduction of taxes on the first 6K of the replacement vehicle. The $580 delta (between $7K private market and $6,420 adjusted trade-in value) may be inconsequential if you don't have enough time to sell it yourself. (Dealing with inquiries, test drives and price negotiations with prospective buyers can be trying.)

- After attaining EFI, if you are flush with cash you may discover you gain greater satisfaction driving more standardly equipped, modest vehicles (i.e., Toyota Camry) over fully loaded luxury ones ( Lexus sedan) costing several thousand dollars more. (Toyota Motor Corp. owns both brands and provides a high degree of quality across all makes and models ... As does General Motors with its Chevrolet and Cadillac divisions and Honda with its regular product line and Acura business.)

In closing, hopefully there will come a time you have so much money, you don't know what to do with it all. Until you reach that point, avoid the temptation to reward yourself with "fancy" cars. Although life is short and money isn't everything - If you are not careful with your expenditures, especially very expensive ones like cars, you could harm your financial well-being and jeopardize the attainment of EFI. Therefore, curb your transportation costs by: Foregoing car ownership as long as practical, living below your transportation means by selecting a reasonably priced functional ride that safely and reliably gets you from Point A to Point B and "investing the difference" to minimize opportunity costs. Additionally, saving on transportation is even more productive if you know what to focus on, can negotiate well and accept that in the long run, material things don't lead to happiness.

Attaining EFI is amazingly liberating. Having surplus money in the bank brings peace of mind, among other things. This is markedly true the older you get as your focus shifts towards your non-working retirement years. No one knows how long their passive retirement income needs to last. What if you end up living into your eighties or nineties? Although there are no guarantees, if you build a **sturdy personal frame** you should be in great shape. Just as there are plenty of well-built homes that have stood the test of time for 8 plus decades, there are plenty of octogenarians living today that still have their finances in order. A large majority of them were able to do so, as products of the Great Depression who needed to live frugally and conserve, by properly managing their lifelong expenditures on the top three necessities/essentials (food, housing and transportation) well enough to keep their "Quality Roofs" in place.

# Phase III

The Final Stages - Constructing a Quality Roof:

(Full Maturation and Family Growth - Enjoying Life's Luxuries)

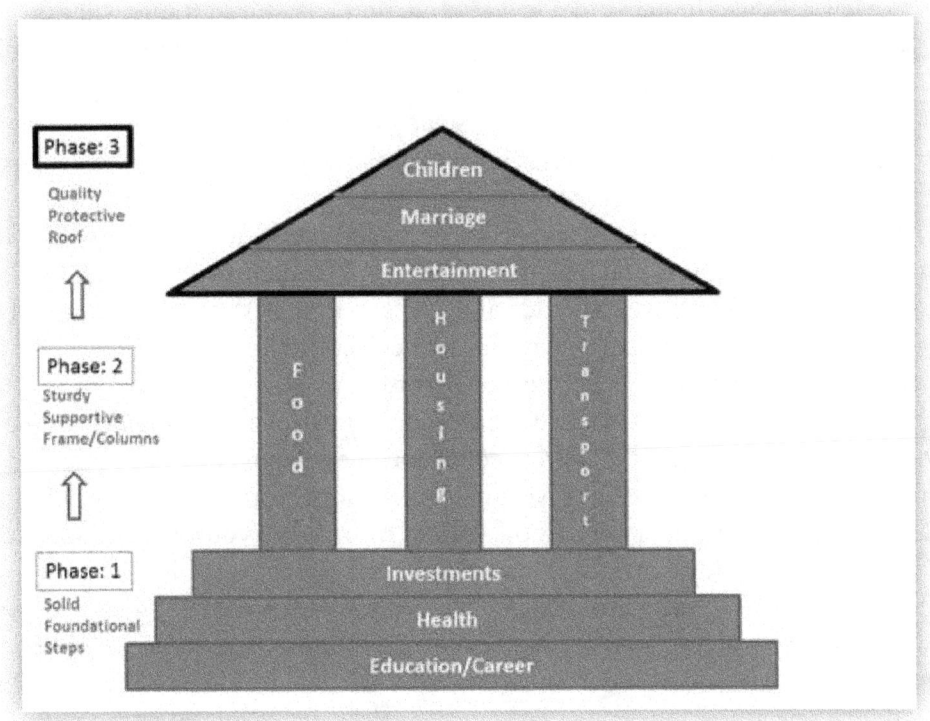

Building & maintaining EFI by managing your "spend"/focus on your personal roof.

A well designed home with a solid foundation and sturdy frame will not stand the test of time without a quality roof that keeps damaging elements at bay. If you cut corners on the roofing installation and use inferior supplies - Rain, ice and snow can weaken the rest of the structure resulting in its total destruction over time, whether by rot, mold infestation or complete collapse onto its occupants and possessions.

Protection and sustainability is the name of the game at this stage. After having made amazing sacrifices laying a solid **"personal foundation"** and establishing a sturdy **"personal frame"** over a decade and a half or more - Why let up now and risk losing all that you have worked so hard for by neglecting the final three key cost saving categories that comprise your **"personal roof"**?

When you are firmly entrenched in living on your own and saving decent money in the process, thanks in part to a great education and job, you must be careful not to squander away your money by: 1) Keeping a close watch on Entertainment/Service expenditures, 2) Marrying a compatible spouse who shares your respect for money, and 3) Raising your children with the same financial values you hold.

Succeeding at this stage and constructing a quality personal roof goes a long way towards ensuring you and your loved ones (namely, your future spouse, children and extended family) are sheltered from damaging financial storms and continue down the path of a rewarding retirement without financial worries. Nothing can negatively disrupt your savings pool more quickly than a gambling addiction, mismatched spouse or needy adult children as the final three chapters will cover.

# CHAPTER 7

## Entertainment/Non-Essential Services

*Living within or below your means includes doing without. (Not just a matter of saving on purchases.)*

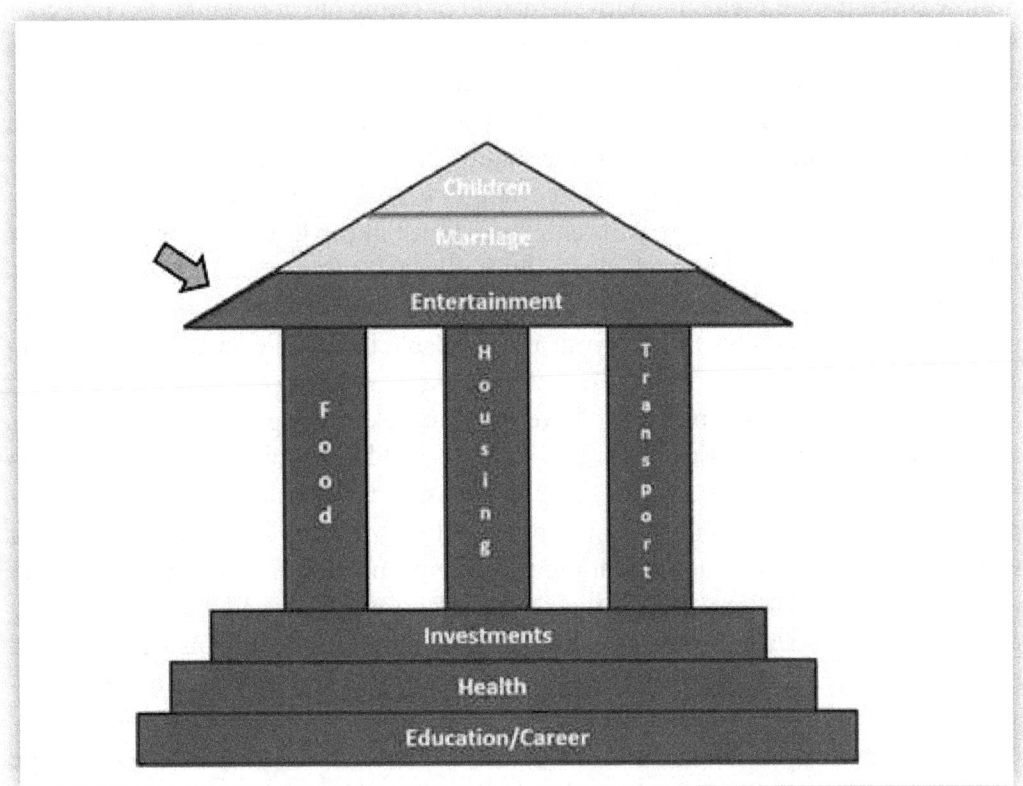

Building & maintaining EFI by managing your "spend"/focus on entertainment/services.

## A. Doing Without - "Made Easy"

Nowhere is this principle easier to apply than with Entertainment and other non-essential expenditures. When starting your quest towards Early Financial Independence (EFI) - This is the one savings category, above and beyond all others you should spend the least amount of your disposable income on.

The six categories reviewed so far (education, health, investing, food, housing and transportation) have all been for **essential/necessary** (non-discretionary) purchases or lifestyle choices. You can't live well and execute a sound savings plan if you don't take your studies or health seriously. And, you certainly can't go very far without food in your stomach and a roof over your head. You need these for survival and can only cut back so far ... i.e., rice and beans over hamburgers; a one room studio apartment over a larger residence.

However, it is *not* essential/necessary for surviving and thriving to spend money on eating out, movie-going, vacationing or attending a ballgame. There are plenty of no/low cost entertainment alternatives. Instead of eating out at restaurants, cook your own meals at home. In lieu of viewing movies in a public theater, rent them for free or a nominal fee from your local library and watch them from home. Vacations can be passed up for relaxing "staycations" and your favorite sports team can be seen in action on TV/cable as opposed to at the stadium. And, the list goes on and on.

If you forgo the right things in your younger years, you should be able to accelerate your savings and maximize your entertainment fun (by leveraging the services of others to free up more time) when you hit your peak earning years. It is usually by then that you have built up a sufficient nest egg and can afford to reward yourself with purchases in this category to keep your rechargeable batteries energized for earning additional income.

We all want to be pampered and have fun. But, acknowledge there are huge costs associated with doing so. Entertainment expenses are like a sink hole. If you step too far in (head first or both feet at the same time), your hard earned savings may disappear forever. Too many hobbies, for example, golfing with club memberships, boating with marina docking fees and attending sporting events as a season ticketholder can drain your bank account when all their ancillary costs/fees are added up ... such as parking, tolls, extra meals out, etc. So pick your entertainment spots carefully and consider opting first to pay for non-essential services that free up your time (not consume it) and improve your quality of life.

Time is money and then some! It may make more sense in your productive wage earning years to pay others to care for your lawn, clean your home and iron/launder your business garments. That way you can spend more time with your career, spouse and children. Increased earnings fuel additional savings and kids aren't kids forever. Before you know it, they will be all grown up. And, you'll be retired with more time on your hands to "in-source" so you can do more for yourself again, without any major regrets.

Don't deprive yourself too much in the way of entertainment/services. It's important to reward yourself along the way, taking time to smell the coffee/flowers. If you're too austere in your savings measures, it may be difficult to stick to a sensible budget. It is human nature to crave what we don't have and – winning the war is most important, not each and every battle brought on by temptation or temporary hardship. Keep yourself anchored (more on that later). It's ok to "sway" occasionally in the sea of life, quite another thing to drift off aimlessly in unknown waters.

Two of the most common entertainment areas to focus reducing your spending on are dining out and taking vacations.

## B. Dining Out in Affordable Fashion

Eating out can be a costly and unhealthy endeavor. Costly, since if you are going to have someone else perform your dirty work (preparing, cooking, serving and cleaning up after your meals) - you are going to have to pay for those services ... Plain and simple. There are no free lunches in life. Learn how to cook and you will save money and eat a lot healthier in the process. Restaurants are notorious for using too much salt, sugar and fat to make their meals irresistible. Not a big deal when consumed infrequently, but quite another if done with regularity.

Tips on saving "dining out" money:

- *Make eating at home the norm and learn to cook.* – Preparing your own meals can be a fun hobby and will reduce your reliance on restaurants. Plus, your future dates and spouse will love you for it.
- *Stick to the main menu.* Make water your beverage of choice and eat appetizers and dessert at home. If you need a reminder why - see Chapter 4 on the linkage of good health to earnings/savings power. (Plus, the highest markups are on drinks, appetizers and desserts.) If your sweet tooth needs satisfying, stop by a bakery on the way home and get a whole pie for the price of two or three dessert items.
- *Use frequent dining cards and coupons whenever possible.* In return for your loyalty/repeat business, many restaurants will reward you with savings the more you dine with them. Also, look on-line for dining discounts from the likes of Restaurant.com, Groupon or BOGO (buy one get one free or ½ off) coupons in your local newspaper or advertising mailers.
- *Favor take-out/pickup over eat in.* Doing so saves time and money, especially the former if you and your spouse both work. Picking up pre-ordered pizzas,

Chinese food or drive through burgers on your commute home is convenient and more economical than dining in, where tips are expected and there is the temptation to order drinks, appetizers and desserts.

- *Consider BYOB establishments over those with liquor licenses.* When dining out and intending to drink alcohol, "Bring Your Own Booze" (BYOB) places can be a very cost effective option. A $10 bottle of wine from your local liquor store provides 4 servings. The same bottle purchased at a moderately priced restaurant with a full service bar may cost $30.00 or $8 per glass. Why not bring your own wine and take the unconsumed portion home?
- *Steer clear of friends/couples with lavish tastes.* It's not a good idea to regularly socialize with dinner dates that like five star restaurants or $100 bottles of wine. There is a tendency in all of us to emulate those we like. And, who we hang out with can influence/re-shape our attitudes and actions, sometimes for the worse.

## C. Vacationing for Less

In your early years, infrequently vacation. This type of activity is a luxury, especially when nights away from home are required. In the "old" days when folks were less caught up in the entitlement mentality, they rarely if ever vacationed even though they could "afford" it. Anyone who has ever lived through the Great Depression, or known someone who has, tends to value having money in the bank over other pursuits.

Tips on saving vacation related money:

- *Leverage day trips as much as possible.* Day trips can be as rewarding as traditional overnight vacations at a fraction of the cost. Explore by car, train or bus, "local" destinations as far as you can travel and return home at night to save on hotel expenses. Note: Using your own car is much more affordable when taking multiple people on a journey. If you are traveling alone and going a long distance, public transportation is usually the way to go.
- *Buy direct.* By eliminating the middle person, you can often save additional money. Purchasing a cruise directly from the cruise line operator can reap savings. And if everything is a push, you may get a free room upgrade or other perk since they have more control over the matter.
- *Obtain at least three price quotes.* As with other purchases, it is important to compare airfare, hotel and rental car rates with other price quotes to stretch your savings. And, if necessary, ask your preferred vendor to beat or at least match your lowest quote. Tip: Vacation packages are worth exploring, because of the economies of scale realized by some sellers through moving large volumes. (I

once went to London for far less than it would have cost if I purchased the air and lodging separately.)
- *Timing is important.* Historically, the best buys on vacations, especially cruises, are in early September when school resumes again and the first two weeks in December. Why early December? Many consumers are forced into savings mode after their Thanksgiving Day travels and are conserving for Christmas and Chanukah gifts or trips. Additionally, early January is an excellent time, depending upon the destination, since many folks tend to over-spend for the holidays and suffer buyer's remorse after seeing their credit card bills. The same can be said for periods of recession, when trips can be significantly slashed. (I travelled to Alaska in 2009 when our economy was still reeling from a major economic downturn and saved 70-80% off an August cruise, primetime for that region.)
- *Stay away from time shares.* Why pay a premium to be locked into the same destination for years on end? Sure, you can trade/swap your unit with other owners to experience different destinations. But why bother? Half the fun of traveling is the planning and "sampling" part ... deciding what to see and for how long (sometimes spur of the moment) without having to stay in one place all week. If you are inclined to purchase a time share, read the fine print. You may be on the hook for yearly maintenance fees subject to rate increases based on the condition of the building. (Not just a one-time upfront fee.)
- *Eat a big breakfast.* And, you can usually skip lunch. This allows more time for sightseeing, when combined with portable on-the-go snacks/refreshments (like sports bars, pretzels, homemade trail mix, juice boxes and refillable water bottles) and makes for a more rewarding dinner.

## D. Staying Anchored By:
Heeding the following advice, particularly in the pursuit of fun and pleasure, so you don't drift away from EFI:

- *Base purchase decisions on your own needs.* You have no one to impress but yourself. Neighbors, friends and family are more focused on their own issues, wants and goals. And, because most people have jealous tendencies, you may do more harm than good to those relationships by being the "top dog". Even if you can easily afford to rent a 6 bedroom shorefront mansion on an exclusive beach all summer, why not opt for a lesser rental and bank the difference? Or, if fast cars are your idea of fun – Consider passing up on a fully loaded Corvette and opting for a comfortably equipped Camaro or Mustang instead.

- *Don't expect help from others.* The only person you can count on for financial assistance is yourself. If you overspend on anything with the belief that friends or family will bail you out should you get in over your head – You are making a grave mistake. Why should others right your wrongs? And, what if they want to, but can't afford to? (Might jeopardize their retirement plans.) The same logic applies to inheritance. Don't spend it in advance. If you are expecting to be willed "x" dollars, but receive a much lesser amount in "y", can you live with the circumstances? If you get a true gift, consider yourself fortunate and be appreciative. Financial assistance usually comes with strings attached, such as interest payments, use of your possessions or other indebtedness with potentially unspecified, vague or unfair terms that can quickly sour good relationships.
- *Stay away from life's top three vices.* Excessive consumption of alcohol, uncontrollable gambling and adultery are home wreckers and can siphon away your savings in short order. Not being able to keep your family together is usually the beginning of the end for EFI. (More to come on that in the next chapter.) If you drink, do so in moderation. The same applies to gambling. Stick to a strict budget and don't exceed it. Believing you can get rich quick or beat the house over the long haul to win back losses is delusional. They don't build large, stylish casinos on house losses, do they? What makes you think you are any different from the average gambler?
- *Maintaining faith in a higher power/spirit.* Finding your religion can keep you on the straight and narrow and shield you from temptation (i.e., the top 3 vices and then some). Having a deep faith or belief in something far more powerful than mere possessions or the fleeting status they may bring, greatly aides in recognizing that "A life devoted to things is a dead life, a stump; a God-shaped life is a flourishing tree." Proverbs 11:28 (MSG).

## E. Successful "On Topic" Savings Techniques with Broad Applicability

You can save serious "dough" on Entertainment and Service related purchases by utilizing the below techniques *and* referring back to previous sections of this guide. The **"7 Ways to Save"** (Chapter 4), **"Not Caring What Others Think"** (Chapter 5) and **"Negotiating Tips"** (Chapter 6) advice are as relevant to this category as they are to food, housing and transportation.

- *Embracing Technology* – The world is rapidly changing and rewards those constantly looking for new ways to save. Paying for a land-line phone service, for example, is a thing of the past. Cell/smart phone coverage in most residential areas is reliable enough to replace your traditional home phone (copper wire infrastructure). And, if you prefer to limit cell phone usage (due to health, cost or convenience concerns), "free" Voice over Internet Protocol (VoIP) phone service can be enjoyed from such providers as Ooma or Skype.

- *Leveraging the Internet* - Brick and mortar retail stores have higher overhead costs than on-line retailers and therefore can't compete with them on offering deeply discounted items. The internet is extremely efficient at identifying smart buys via powerful price comparison engines. Sites like Amazon, e-Bay, Groupon, Travelocity and Priceline, to name a few, are "game changers" and worth keeping close tabs on when Entertainment and Service needs arise. However, before making on-line purchases, ensure the seller is trustworthy based on posted reviews. If an on-line retailer's reputation is "spotty" or suspect and or a deal seems too good to be true, don't do business with them.
- *Shunning Sales Gimmicks* - If asked to make an immediate purchase decision or else the offer is off the table in short order (i.e., in a few minutes or hours), run, don't walk! Pressure tactics are not used by reputable vendors. If a deal is truly a deal, what harm is there in giving you enough time to weigh your options? Those who sell time shares or wholesale travel club services are notorious for using such methods to prey on consumers blinded by emotion or ill equipped to fend off seasoned sales pros with the upper hand/"home field advantage". Other signs you are in for trouble: If the vendor will not supply you with documents to review in advance or no rescission period language exists in the contract. You need time to analyze major purchase decisions to ensure they are right for you and deliver real value.
- *Adopting a Pre-Tax Mindset* - When analyzing purchase decisions, think about what an item or service costs in terms of pre-tax dollars/wages. This approach should make you second guess or re-evaluate, for good cause, a variety of expenditures. For instance, adding a $20 music CD to your personal collection, depending on your tax bracket, might mean you have to earn $30 to acquire it. You may come to the realization you don't need the entire CD as it only has one great song on it. And, you are better served listening to that one song on the radio or downloading it to a personal device for $1.29. (Only pay for what you need.) Compulsion and convenience will cost you in the long run. If you don't learn to practice restraint when you are young, you may not be able to do so when you get older and bigger, more expensive toys are within realistic reach (large screen TVs, boats, luxury homes, etc.).
- *Factoring Operating and Maintenance Costs into the Affordability Equation* – Although this was previously reviewed in the context of housing, it bears

repeating. Can you afford to operate and maintain the item you are purchasing? A used boat might cost 50K, which you may be able to cover with plenty of cushion. But, can you afford year after year the fuel, docking fees, insurance and engine/equipment tune-up costs to keep the boat fully operational? (These costs might run several thousand dollars per year, eating into your savings rate.) Golfing is another example where high recurring costs come into play. The clubs and balls are affordable enough, but what about the time commitment (4 plus hours per round), green fees, rental carts, practice sessions and possible club membership with mandatory minimum meal expenditures? To properly assess affordability, perform a **TOTAL** cost of ownership analysis before making big commitments so there are no hidden surprises. How would you feel surrendering your boat or golf membership at a fraction of what you paid, because you couldn't afford the up-keep?

- *Living a "Less is More" Lifestyle* – Do you really need that stamp, rock, sea shell, shot glass, crystal figurine, sports memorabilia, coin, comic book, "you name it" collection? Why not leave that to museums or other entities thrilled to have you admire theirs, which are usually much more extensive? The same applies to having expensive hobbies. Pick one or two, invest in the right essential tools without being extravagant, and use common sense to guide your decisions. If you love photography – Do you really need multiple cameras with multiple lenses? Or, your own dark room? Not in today's digital age, where a solid camera can be had for a reasonable price and individual shots can be uploaded directly to a computer with photo shop editing capabilities. Main message: Resist the urge to buy things you don't need. Ask yourself *before* making a purchase – "What will I do with it? Do I really need this item or will it simply collect dust and add to clutter? Should I borrow or rent it instead? If the item will not change your life in any meaningful way, pass on it. All too often we buy something, because we enjoy the thought of owning it more than actually using or admiring it.

- *Considering Opportunity Costs at Every Turn* (worth repeating) –Is as applicable to entertainment/service expenditure decisions as those dealing with education, investment and transportation. When evaluating entertainment purchases, like installing an in-ground swimming pool at home, instead of joining a local swim club - consider what you are forgoing by doing so. The initial 50K outlay on a pool's construction, plus increased annual property taxes, pool supplies and opening/closing costs if invested in an index fund and left untouched for 2 decades, could very well produce a stash of $1,000,000 or more. What do you think your pool will be worth after twenty years? (Not sure it even increases the value of your home.) Note: A private pool's upkeep and chemicals can easily cost $1000 a summer (3 months) versus $400 for a seasonal membership of the same length at a local public swim club. Ask before making significant purchases - What else could or should I be doing with my money so EFI will be more attainable?

- *Keeping Your Current Provider Honest* –Not only applies to automobile mechanics (covered earlier), but also utility, phone and cable TV providers. By checking competitor's prices from time to time, you'll minimize being taken advantage of. It is easy to become complacent if your current provider is doing a nice job servicing you. Remember, however, their primary interest is making as much profit as possible, not putting money back in your pocket. With regard to cable service, for example, when your bundle or special pricing expires, be proactive and inquire about new specials. If there are none, ask them to match the price of a competitor's promotion or you might consider leaving. You will learn more often than not, your request will be granted. **If you don't ask, you don't receive.**

- *Using Cash Whenever Practical* - When you see real money (paper currency) leaving your wallet during purchase transactions, it will make you think twice about what you are doing. It's easier to "get in over your head" when you swipe your charge card, since you don't feel the loss until much later. (Separation of cause and effect.) Spending $200 apiece for discounted courtside basketball seats may have seemed like the fun and reasonable thing to do at the time. However, if you charged them to your credit card, you may have a very different feeling when you settle your monthly bill. Note: Credit card companies always prefer you carry a balance so you have to pay them costly interest. Don't succumb to this with discretionary entertainment expenses. Instead, reserve paying credit card interest for true emergencies, like getting by without a job or tending to personal health issues that can't go untreated.

## F. Miscellaneous Considerations:

- Rent, stream or download "older" movies and watch them from home. Attending movie theatres on a regular basis can get expensive. Their ticket prices are high, as are the markups on their food and beverages. If you can abstain from viewing new releases for a while, everything will eventually seem new to you and then you can watch them on the cheap via rentable CD or pay per view. Sure, a night out with friends or a date is more exciting at a big screen theater, but you can still reduce costs by using discounted movie vouchers. These are usually available in Entertainment Books or through

employer group purchase discount programs. And, attending matinees (first showings of the day) are always an affordable option.
- Instead of joining a gym, create your own in-home fitness center. Working out will be much cheaper, far more convenient and less time consuming if you do so, which in turn might translate into working out more often and improved health. (You'd be surprised what you can do with 1 multi-purpose machine.) Attending a public gym requires making yourself somewhat "presentable" (newer workout attire), spending time and gas travelling to/from and resisting the urge to strike up conversations when you are in a rush. If limited space at home is holding you back, why not purchase a small treadmill or bike for aerobic activity and a few free weights for building/maintaining body strength? If you need to be around others for motivation or are looking to meet that someone special, who shares in your enthusiasm for staying fit, consider joining a local running or biking club.
- You don't need to spend a small fortune to have well-groomed hair. Instead of patronizing a fancy salon, try the services of a no-frills barber where prices tend to be quite reasonable. If you are dissatisfied with the results, try another barber at the same shop or a nearby location. A haircutter's ability can vary greatly based on training and experience. Should barber shops ever become extinct (a distinct possibility), family oriented hair salon franchises offer a decent product at a decent price with or without appointments and limited wait times. Tip: To extend time between cuts, have someone shave the back of your neck line (remove stray hairs) and if applicable, trim your bangs and sideburns with an electric razor.
- Learn to iron your clothes. There will be occasions you are away from home and need to "spot treat" previously unwrinkled garments with a guest/hotel iron. (For business meetings, an important interview or special event such as a wedding.) If your hotel is unable to steam/press your garment(s) in time for the event, knowing how to iron, besides saving money, will ensure you always look presentable. Some dry cleaning expenses are unavoidable, such as with suits and fine slacks. However, for business casual meetings, consider purchasing iron-free dress pants that don't require dry cleaning. Be sure to spend extra on a good quality pair. Your clients and co-workers can spot the cheap polyester ones a mile away.
- Limit the purchase of expensive jewelry and watches ... a form of entertainment of sorts. In today's era of increasing poverty, which is only going to worsen as globalization continues to mature and wreak havoc on our overpaid workforce – Being ostentatious is risky behavior. Doing so is like wearing a bull's eye around your neck for those less fortunate that must do whatever

it takes to survive. Don't tempt others while attempting to bolster your self-esteem. One solid watch is all you need for work and fancy jewelry and accessories don't make "The Man/Woman". Instead, confidence, compassion, intellect and achievement are among the mark of having arrived, not some flashy logo, shiny gold chain or sparkling rock. (More on diamonds in the next section.)

In review: If you can't afford something, don't buy it, especially as it relates to this chapter's savings category. Debt is something you should avoid whenever possible. Get into the habit of asking yourself – Is this entertainment/service expense absolutely essential? If not, pass up on it until you can well afford it. Doing without *non-essentials* is easier than you think.

When you are ready to enjoy the luxury of traveling and having others wait on you, learn how to vacation for less and dine out in affordable fashion by staying anchored and applying the time tested savings techniques covered herein. You will be glad you did, as you construct a quality personal leak-proof roof that protects you and your loved ones for many years on end!

# CHAPTER 8

## Marriage/Friends

*Take ample time to get to know your future lifelong partner. Marriage is a legally binding contract with potentially severe financial consequences should it be broken.*

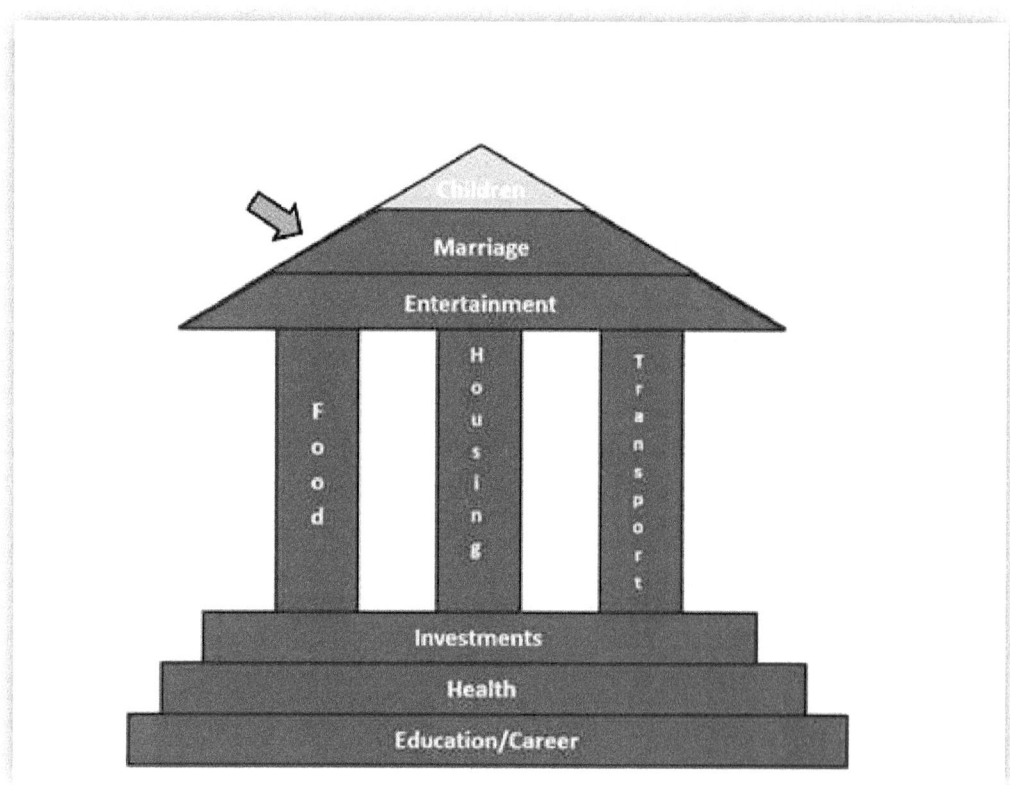

Building & maintaining EFI by managing your "spend"/focus on your marriage/friends.

## A. Financial Impact of Relationships – "For Better or For Worse"

Who you associate with can make or break you from a savings standpoint. The beliefs, attitudes and actions of your friends, family and significant other/spouse all influence you to a large extent. It's human nature to become more like those we spend time with. And, what we think often gets acted upon. If your "circle of influence" is loose with money (i.e., gambling, drug or alcohol addictions or just undisciplined), there is a good chance it will rub off on you.

Be selective with who you hang out with, opting for quality relationships over quantity. In today's era of social networking (Facebook, MySpace, Twitter, etc.) it's easy to mistake acquaintances for friends. Therefore, make the most of your free time by spending it with "good" people who share and reinforce your core values, including having a healthy respect for money and the importance of saving. Aside from being quite expensive, certain vices/behaviors can be emotionally and physically devastating (wreaking untold havoc on personal lives) and are not easy to break until you hit rock bottom. When in doubt about someone, look at their friends. Birds of a feather tend to flock together.

Who you date and ultimately marry has, by far and away, the largest impact on your financial well-being than any other relationship. Marrying the right spouse can accelerate your savings efforts many fold. Marrying the wrong one, however, could single-handedly destroy your chances of accumulating wealth and achieving Early Financial Independence. If your partner is wasteful, irresponsible or materialistic, they can drive you into bankruptcy since their debt is your debt. And, typically the further into a relationship you proceed (i.e., having a house and kids) before it falls apart, the more money you stand to lose. Alimony, child support and dividing everything in half can be an expensive proposition as covered shortly.

Although who you marry is a *very* unique and personal decision ... and you can't always control who you fall in love with ... don't leave it to chance with an "I'll know it when it feels right" approach. If you have not given *considerable* advance thought about what your ideal partner should embody in terms of essential traits/characteristics, don't get married! Failure to do so increases the odds you will fall in love with the wrong person (love is blind) and your marriage will end prematurely due to lack of compatibility. The less *key* areas you have in common with your partner, the worse off you'll likely be. (More on commonality, the relationship "glue" later.)

Unfortunately, love alone is not enough to prevail from a marriage standpoint when your relationship is stress tested and fails. As hard and unpopular as this may be to hear – Walk away from a mismatched partner ***before*** you tie the knot, even if you love them dearly and vice versa. (Better yet, don't even date them for fun in the first place if they don't meet certain criteria, since you can be easily swayed by infatuation/love.) The pain of the initial separation may be severe, but it will be nowhere near as debilitating as parting ways after you say "I do" and kids are involved.

Putting money issues aside - Bad marriages are toxic emotionally and physically and, this toxicity can extend well beyond their formal dissolution. What if the late Whitney Houston, arguably the greatest female vocalist of all time, had instead married someone of the caliber of a Kevin Costner? She *may* not have gotten involved with drugs (her demise) and might very well still be with us today. I use Whitney as an example, because she passed away at a fairly young age (48) and was laid to rest in the same cemetery as my Mom a short 4 months later. Whitney's passing reinforced to me (based on reading certain allegedly true news accounts about her life and marriage struggles) the importance of selecting the right mate the first time around, since the wrong one can destroy your chances at EFI *and so much more*.

## B. Are You Commitment-Worthy?

Before putting prospective marriage partners under the microscope, ask yourself - Are you ready for a serious relationship? In other words, are you commitment-worthy? Be honest! If not, you are doing yourself and others a grave disservice. It takes two well-adjusted adults for a long-term partnership to survive. And, the success or failure of that partnership starts with you.

If you have not learned to love, trust and respect **YOURSELF** – What makes you think you can reciprocate with others? You must be able to carry your own emotional weight before entering a marriage. If you are self-absorbed, immature or overly pessimistic, for instance – Work on improving YOU first so your future marriage has a fighting chance of survival. Marriage is difficult enough for individuals adequately prepared to reap its rewards. (Close to 50% of all marriages in the United States end in divorce.) Why make yours any more likely to fail?

And, realize timing is a big part of the overall commitment equation. Even if you are emotionally ready for marriage, if your primary focus is obtaining a degree or establishing a career, a serious relationship may not be in the cards for a while. A serious relationship can distract from achieving major goals requiring you to be "all in". Not to say you can't simultaneously date and establish a solid foundation for future monetary success. It depends on your personality and ability to juggle multiple balls in the air at once. Some folks are adept at doing so, others are not so fortunate. Knowing yourself and your limits is an important element in making sound decisions.

Don't let age alone be a factor in deciding if you are commitment worthy. Although it's not optimal to get married too early or too late in life, the worst thing you can do is let age rush you into a decision. If your goal has always been to wed at 25, and you are not marriage material by then, take more time to find yourself. What harm is there in waiting a few years? There is more harm in making the wrong choice, than waiting to make the right one.

Don't be afraid to marry in your mid to late twenties. Caring for young children is physically taxing and your body will be much better equipped to do so at say 28 than 38. Plus, having to meet their needs (formula, diapers, toys, doctor's visits, pre-school costs, etc.) is expensive and should provide you with extra incentive to advance your career sooner rather than later. Who doesn't want the best for their kids? You will feel the same and do whatever it takes to increase your earnings potential at a time in your life when your efforts still make a big difference.

It's more difficult at 40 with young kids to alter your career path/trajectory than in your 20s. Rising stars are usually given the chance to prove themselves in leadership positions when they are in their late twenties or early thirties. Employees who are 40 plus and have been "stagnating" in lesser jobs (perhaps by putting themselves in a holding pattern, while taking care of young families) are often passed over for promotions, even if they are solid performers. It's best to have kids when you are young; your job responsibilities less taxing and you are more promotable with ample physical energy to conquer it all.

Additionally, if you wait until your late thirties or early forties to marry, all the *great* partners will be gone and you might feel inclined to settle for someone with "baggage". Baggage is a good thing when travelling somewhere overnight. In terms of marriage, it should be avoided like the plague as it increases your odds of getting divorced ... A costly event as explored next.

## C. The High Cost of Divorce

A divorce can sting emotionally and financially. The stress and trauma associated with undoing a marriage can cause mental and physical ills requiring medical and professional attention. (Like battling depression, taking antidepressants and undergoing regular counseling.)

And, if your head's not "in the game" at work while on the mend from a messy split, your job performance will suffer – potentially negatively impacting your earnings power and savings rate. Equally concerning, a divorce can harm the psyche and finances of your ex-spouse, children, parents and other loved ones for years.

Even if you are spared from the emotional side effects of divorce, you will rarely ever be able to say the same about your financial health. Unless you divorce shortly after marriage with few assets and no children, you will most likely be on the hook for lifestyle changing support payments for a long time. Perhaps until you die. Therefore, be highly selective as to whom you marry to avoid creating casualties along the way and to mitigate having to pay the following failed marriage "penalties": Alimony, child support and division of marital property.

*Disclaimer: The below failed marriage penalties review is not intended to serve as legal advice, but rather to open your eyes to potential pitfalls and complexities related to the subjects using my cursory knowledge of NJ law as a baseline to frame out the discussion. A competent licensed attorney specializing in Matrimonial & Family law in your state, jurisdiction or territory should be consulted should you have any questions or concerns about a given topic.*

**Alimony** – Is financial support **you** may have to pay to a *former* marriage partner so they can care for themselves post-divorce. The payments are either temporary or permanent in nature. The former are designed to last just long enough get your ex back on their feet so they can acquire new skills and competencies to be competitive in the job market. (This may entail going back to school.) Unfortunately, if your former spouse is hopelessly inept, too sick or too old to be rehabilitated to enter the workforce, you may be legally obligated to pay alimony until one of you dies or your ex re-marries. And depending on the circumstances, you may end up paying both temporary and permanent alimony with significant time sandwiched in between. (I.e. - Ex gets rehabilitated career wise, has a successful run at it, contracts a major illness and because disability payments are insufficient – obtains a court order for you to pay permanent alimony.) The reality may be - Once your spouse, always your spouse until death separates you.

Although there appear to be no fixed formulas in New Jersey, for instance, for calculating alimony (up to a judge's discretion), the courts must consider 13 factors, including marital lifestyle. (N.J.S.A. 2A:34-23(b)) What this may mean to you – You may be ordered to pay your ex a monthly support figure allowing them to continue living the same lifestyle they enjoyed during your marriage. If you shared a $750,000 dollar home together as husband and wife (or common law companion) and your monthly mortgage payment plus property taxes were in the vicinity of $4,000, you might very well have to continue paying that same amount in alimony … All while having to absorb your own personal housing costs. Carrying two residences, which may include your former marital home if you separate with young kids, can destroy EFI. Judges are reluctant to downsize the accommodations of children in the name of what's in their "best interest" … meaning there could be little income left over to support your housing needs after alimony and child support.

**Child Support** – Is what you may owe your children to continue providing them the same standard of living they enjoyed pre-divorce … whenever *feasible*, until emancipation or beyond. (If you do well, you might be petitioned to assist them with college or graduate school tuition fees and living expenses.) And, what you consider feasible and a judge considers feasible can be polar opposites.

Unlike alimony, child support usually can't be waived or negotiated down. In New Jersey for example, there are fixed mandatory guidelines a court must weigh before arriving at a monthly figure. One such guideline is your income. The more you make, the more you owe. And, therein lies the problem! There is no way to ensure your ex (and if applicable their new partner) does not benefit from your child support payments. Your children's *actual* food, clothing and shelter costs may only be $1,000 a month on the high end, but a judge may nonetheless set their support at $2,000 a month because you earn a decent salary. Where is the extra 1K going? If you don't have primary custody, you'll never know.

No normal parent wants their kids to suffer. And most separating parents realize just because their marriage did not work out, doesn't mean their kids should not be their shared economic responsibility. What hurts the most beyond not being able to see your kids as regularly after the split and potentially benefiting your ex with excesses baked into the child support payments - You can no longer pool your assets to offset fixed living expenses. Instead of 4 people living under one roof, you may have two residences to support - Your new place at 100% and the residence of your kids and ex at x%, which might be a combination of your alimony and child support contributions. Two mortgages and two property tax bills are almost always more expensive than one of each. All this additional expenditure adds up and makes you less desirable to future spouses, since there will be less money for them.

Wait at least two years into marriage before having children, preferably three or four. If things don't work out in your partnership, it will be much easier and far less costly to part ways without children. Failure to pay child support may have major repercussions beyond your kids doing without. If you don't voluntarily make the court ordered payments on a regular basis: 1.Your wages may be garnished through your employer. 2. Your credit score/rating may be harmed, perhaps even destroyed. 3. You may be forced into bankruptcy protection. 4. Could be striped of your hard earned professional licenses and certifications; 5. If you own real estate, a lien might be placed on it for the amount you are in arrears. Main message: You can run, but not successfully hide from your child support obligations. Nor should you. Your kids are your responsibility!

**Division of Community/Marital Property** – If you are married a certain amount of time (ten years or more seems to be the magic number in NJ) you and your spouse may have to split almost everything 50/50. Although physically dividing a house in half is not practical, you may get to keep ½ the proceeds from its sale, one car, the dining room set and your exercise equipment, for example, while you ex keeps the rest ... including your once joint savings account.

Seems fair? It may be in the eyes of The Law and in light of your unique circumstances at the time. But, having to buy everything else, such as new kitchenware, bedroom furniture and other basics can add up fast, all at a time you need to cut back because of possible alimony and child support obligations. And, it may come as a surprise to learn - What you thought was off limits in the event of divorce may not be the case. Your prized baseball card collection, fishing cabin and refurbished muscle car **all acquired pre-marriage with your own assets** may need to be divided evenly if you used any amount of marital money to add to or improve upon them.

In summary, divorce is an expensive proposition. Even if you don't have to pay alimony or child support, parting ways with a former best friend, letting go of sentimental marital property and beginning life anew can be a painful, difficult process. Therefore, be highly selective who you marry to minimize the risk of permanent separation.

Although there is no way to guarantee your marriage will work - Ask yourself *before* getting married: 1) Will your partner likely play fair in the event of divorce? (If you fear getting on their mean side, search no more for an answer.) 2) Can they support themselves without your assistance ... meaning high earning capacity? 3) Do you have enough in common to "stick" together through thick and thin? And, 4) Did they pass the courtship "stress test" so your relationship is somewhat weatherized against future storms? The more "Yes" answers, the more likely things will work out. The next two sections are designed to aid in properly responding to the last two questions.

## D. Commonality – The Relationship "Glue"

The more you have in common with your spouse, the more compatible you will be. The more compatible, the more likely you will stay together with less friction and conflict in your daily interactions.

Commonality breeds harmonious, agreeable and congenial relations - The very definition of compatibility. In other words, it is the adhesive or glue that binds people together. Although there is no sure fire way to pick a spouse that will stand the test of time (no divorce), the more you have in common with regard to basic values, ethics, religion, race, socio-economic background, etc. – the greater chance things will work out. Makes sense, right?

Take note: Love is "blinding" in that it alters our ability to reason. You can be so "in love" and feel so good about someone, that you minimize their weaknesses and can't see the truth clearly. Many folks even contemplate getting married with the mindset they can change what they don't like about their partners. Resist this wishful thinking!! It can't be done. You can't materially change your partner to think or act more like you.

Either you learn to live with them as they presented themselves during courtship or you move on. As a best practice - don't get involved with someone in the first place who doesn't meet your requirements, so you can't be lured in and trapped by love.

There are two commonality categories to pay close attention to while dating. Five *nonnegotiable_ones*, that you should share **everything** in common with your partner as they form the basis of mutual respect, without which your relationship will fail. (Trustworthiness, conservative monetary values, solid work ethic, similar need for affection and shared definition of family.) And, numerous *negotiable ones* that are extremely important, but not relationship breakers if there are some differences.

## Nonnegotiable Commonalities

**1) Trustworthiness** - Is all about honesty and being able to confidently rely upon someone else to do the right thing. If your future spouse is not honest in small matters, what makes you think they will be in larger matters? As it relates to prudently managing money - If your partner routinely spends a lot on fancy clothes, vacations and spa treatments, will they have enough left over to assist with the mortgage or other essentials? If they hide purchases from you while dating, what else might they be hiding from you? Trust pertains to so much more than not cheating on one another. It also means being open about your expenditures and being willing to compromise when there is conflict.

**2) Conservative Monetary Values** - What if your partner is open and honest about purchases, but doesn't value the importance of saving money the way you do? Your marriage may be doomed from the start. Research indicates money trouble is one of the top three reasons marriages fail. (The other two, lack of sharing control in major household decisions and sexual incompatibility.) Think twice about committing to someone who believes wholeheartedly in living for the moment and enjoying life to its fullest *regardless* of the expense. Things don't usually work out in the end unless you plan for them. Hard work and discipline are absolutely necessary for success in any area. If you want EFI bad enough, team up with a life partner who truly shares the same monetary values as you.

How do you test for sincerity in this regard? Casual conversations with your future in-laws should reveal how they really feel about the importance of saving and spending prudently. If they are in alignment with your values, odds are high their offspring (your future spouse) will be as well since the apple usually doesn't fall too far from the tree. If they are not in alignment, take note: There is a greater than average chance that if you marry into their family you will someday be providing your future in-laws with monetary assistance. Should you be funding someone else's retirement when you have your own to save for? (You may not have a say in the matter.)

Closely analyze your partner's actions. If they are constantly trying to keep up with the "Joneses", regardless of how stellar their paycheck is, be careful. The world is full of high income earners routinely spending more than they make. What's the point of earning big bucks, if due to poor spending habits and lack of self-control you have no savings to show for it? There may come a time in life you desperately need to tap into an emergency cash reserve. What if none exists?

**3) Solid Work Ethic** – Entails far more than being the polar opposite of lazy. Someone who possesses this virtue is not only highly reliable, goal oriented and driven by accomplishment, but also willing to put in the time, energy and effort to carry their own weight (and others when needed) at work, home and in their community. Folks with a solid work ethic want to succeed at whatever they do, no matter how small or large a task. They are self-motivated to put in a fair day's work, even when fair pay is not on the line, and genuinely care about their contributions.

A partner who is easy going and generally carefree may be highly appealing to date, but if these traits are also accompanied by irresponsibleness, lack of ambition or inability to care for their own basic needs – run for the hills. A spouse who is unwilling to pitch in with common household chores, child rearing responsibilities or holding down a full time job if your personal finances dictate such, will fracture your marriage. There will come a point in your relationship when you can no longer carry them. And, even if you can – Your lack of respect for them will push you further and further away physically and emotionally, eventually resulting in a dissolved marriage.

**4) Similar Need for "Affection"** - Although it's a given the person you marry must love you (strong emotional affection), many people overlook the importance of sharing the same degree of physical affection to ensure the success of a marriage. Sexual compatibility is more important than you might imagine. And, assuming you are a match in this area, you are not out of the woods if your idea of physical intimacy is a quick rub on the back when your other half needs quality time hugging and holding hands. Dating is the best time to test emotional and physical compatibility. (Realize with regard to the latter, how far you go is highly personal based on your shared religious, moral and personal convictions.). What happens if after you tie the knot you realize you aren't a good match for "affection"? Again, sex, money and control issues are the three main reasons marriages fail.

**5) Shared Definition of Family** – If your idea of the ideal family consists of a spouse and dog, while your partner couldn't feel whole or complete without a child or two – Put the wedding on hold. Some partners can become so consumed by the biological urge to experience parenthood that nothing can stand in their way of fulfilling this need. You might be able to delay the inevitable by kicking the "can" down the road for years on end. Eventually, however, the desire to raise prodigy will become so strong you will be forced to make a tough choice … Either satisfy your partner's wishes or part ways. You may think you can successfully substitute having children for something else, but you can't. Make absolutely sure you share the same views on having children before marriage. Lack of agreement on this subject after you exchange vows spells major trouble.

On a related note: Wait at least two years after getting married before having kids. That way you can feel things out and get to know your partner better, building up emotional deposits along the way. Kids have a way of straining marriages, leaving little time for couples to strengthen their bonds. If yours is already strained short of the breaking point before introducing kids into the equation, delay having them and seek professional counseling. If your marital problems can't be fixed after a reasonable attempt to patch things up, file for divorce. Your future kids don't deserve the turmoil and major disruptions divorce will thrust upon them. And, divorce is much messier and far more complicated when you have children. You will forever have to interact with your ex when it comes to coordinating custody visits, support payments and attending certain events (child's back-to-school nights, concerts, sports competitions, graduations, wedding, etc.). If your marriage is going to fail, let it fail fast and move on!

The above non-negotiable commonalities form a strong chain. If just one of them is a weak link in your marital relationship – "Game over" is highly likely. They collectively form the basis of *mutual respect*. If you don't share the same general level of trustworthiness, monetary values, work ethic, physical and emotional needs and shared definition of family – You will eventually lack respect for one another. Without respect a marriage can't succeed.

Money can't buy respect. Nor, should it serve as the basis for selecting a mate. Sure, it can be the fastest way to becoming rich. But exchanging vows with a wealthy spouse is no guarantee their wealth will become your wealth. Your wealthier half may not have control over their money. (A legal trustee may be appointed by their family to determine how it is distributed and spent.) And, your spouse may decide to keep their finances separate through a pre-nuptial agreement (more on that later) or informally through separate bank accounts. You will initially like the money, but if you lack true respect for your spouse – It will eventually drive you away and you may have nothing or little to show for your time spent together.

## Negotiable Commonalities

Negotiable commonalities are as important to assess as nonnegotiable ones. Minor differences in enough areas can cumulatively fester into major issues, resulting in large stress fractures in your relationship.

**Income Generating Capabilities & Career Mindedness** – Are you counting on two incomes to live a certain lifestyle? If so, selecting a partner with good career prospects and high earning potential is something to weigh. In today's economic climate, the reality is it takes two incomes in most regions of the country to live comfortably and to be able to save for EFI.

If your spouse intends to work at the inception of marriage – Do they plan to stop temporarily or permanently to rear your children? If the latter, don't factor their income into any mortgage affordability equations. You may not be able to count on their financial contributions for very long. (Note: A stay at home partner performs noble services that can't be bought. Nonetheless, integrating this type of arrangement into your household structure is a luxury. If you can afford to do so - Congratulations! But, also understand the ramifications of decreased retirement and college savings and perhaps delayed EFI if you pursue the single household income earner route.)

**Religion** - Or spirituality, plays a part in our beliefs and values. Choosing a spouse with a different religion (or no religion at all, as in agnostic or atheist) can cause added marital friction. How would you feel if your spouse insisted on having you or your children limit or abstain from outwardly celebrating the very holidays and convictions that make you who you are?

Lack of commonality in religion does not ordinarily make-or-break a relationship. However, it may increase your risk for divorce. An often quoted article reports, "According to calculations based on the American Religious Identification Survey of 2001, people who had been in mixed-religion marriages were three times more likely to be divorced or separated than those who were in same-religion marriages." (Riley, Naomi Schaefer, "Love conquers all Except religion", June 6, 2010, *The Washington Post*, Washington, DC).

Although religion can be a powerful unifying and healing force, it can cause conflict even when you share the same exact religious affiliation or denomination as your partner. If your partner believes in tithing a significant portion of your income to the church and you disagree – Discord may follow. Just as being forced to attend worship services on a weekly basis, when your commitment level is more in the once a month or major holidays only range.

**Socio Economic Status** – Is someone's standing in society based on their income, education and occupation/career attainments. If your future in-laws rank much less than you in these categories – You may be funding them at some point in your marriage. Conversely, if they have much more than you and your family, you may not be able to live up to their expectations of being able to provide your children with the same standard of living, education, etc. your prospective spouse enjoyed growing up.

And, if you are ultimately supported or propped up by your in-laws, you may eventually feel very awkward or uncomfortable about the situation ... Especially if they don't like you, because you don't show the expected level of appreciation or compliance to their rules. Gifted money often comes with strings attached, such as the need for control and involvement in your personal affairs.

There are numerous benefits to marrying within your "class", like having more in common with your partner based on similar childhood experiences, viewpoints and family interactions that could potentially result in a tighter marital bond.

**Descent, Country of Origin/Nationality & Race** – Are all powerful contributors in defining how we think and act. They give us a sense of much needed identity in a large, diverse world. Thus, where your partner's ancestors/roots are from, their country of origin and how closely they identify with their native culture and race will impact your relationship. It's only a matter of to what extent!

And, place of birth is too limiting of a factor to focus on. A partner born in New Jersey to parents who immigrated to the United States from Argentina (their birthplace), for instance, may have genetic links to three continents, but more closely identify with their rich African heritage, which you will need to embrace ... at a minimum, for the good of the marriage.

Some additional thoughts: Regardless of where your partner's roots are from – Can you accept their family's cultural traditions, many of which may involve sharing in ethnic food? Are you interested in visiting their country of origin and learning more about their background? Are you hoping your future children adopt certain aspects of your future in-laws way of life or pride of nationality? If you answered "no" to any of these, you need to think about how this will impact your relationship. When marrying someone different from you, it is best to embrace their culture/race/etc., rather than just "tolerate" this facet of them and their family. Otherwise, it adds another point of friction in your relationship that extends to children and in-laws.

When you get married, your spouse's family becomes your family and vice versa. If you don't respect and take a sincere interest in your future in-laws descent, nationality and race – What makes you think there will ever be harmony in your relationship with your spouse? Hosting a family gathering can be stressful enough when everything is in perfect order. When there are major underlying differences as to the foods that should be served, music played and style of dance/celebration/customs displayed - additional disagreements and stress can arise.

Think twice about marrying someone who may be after your citizenship. There is a chance a non-citizen may be marrying you solely to permanently reside in the United States. (When does their green card or Visa expire?) Once the legal waiting period is up, their intentions may be to leave you. And, should your need to annul or divorce and child custody is in dispute, your partner might return to their native homeland with your kids and you may never see them again ... Even though their actions were illegal.

Parting thought on this subject. You may be able to take your partner out of their "homeland", but you can't take the "homeland" out of your partner. Accept them for whom they are and respect their differences.

**Physical Attractiveness** – Is an important consideration. You must be physically attracted to your spouse and vice versa for your marriage to work. It all boils down to basic biology and the "birds and the bees". You may think you are way different than other animals on this planet, but you are actually very similar to them. You must eat, drink and sleep to survive ... And, you are instinctively motivated to seek shelter from the elements, mate/reproduce and protect your possessions and family.

If your partner is only somewhat into you from a looks standpoint and/or you and your partner are not equally attractive (or at least in the same ballpark), the imbalance can strain your relationship. A woman, for instance, that is far more beautiful than her man is handsome is settling for some reason. That reason may be for extra financial support, emotional stability or enhanced physical well-being for her and her family. Her reasons for settling may be reasonable. But, what if the man can't fully accommodate them? If he doesn't deliver his end of the unspoken bargain, his marriage will suffer casualties.

Resist the temptation to land a "trophy spouse" if your looks alone don't warrant such. Although having a trophy by your side may signal you have arrived in the eyes of others, they are costly to maintain emotionally and financially. Physical attractiveness fades over time (both literally and figuratively) and when your infatuation wanes, you may not be so keen on paying for their high maintenance lifestyle. Ask yourself - Can you afford what your prospective spouse may be accustomed to enjoying or wants to enjoy? Even if they say they can cut back during marriage, have they been able to do so for sustained periods of time during your courtship? Is your partner physically attracted to you or feigning it for opportunistic reasons?

**Education/Intelligence Levels** – Maintaining a successful marriage is a lot like running a profitable business. If one spouse doesn't carry their weight in certain "departments" the other must pick up the slack or the entire organization suffers. Household procurement decisions requiring a thorough analysis of your unique needs, circumstances and goals (i.e., what car, house or investments to purchase) demand a certain degree of brainpower to execute properly. Therefore, it's almost a necessity to marry someone who is smart (high IQ or emotional intelligence) and equally educationally accomplished to aid in making tough decisions and keeping stress levels in check.

Also, being able to carry on stimulating conversations with your spouse is extremely important and rewarding. "Communication problems" were the leading cause of divorce per a 2012 survey of counseling professionals at YourTango.com – The self-proclaimed "digital leader in love and relationships." And, I can't think of any other leisure activity you might mutually engage in more frequently than the pleasure of exchanging free flowing emotions, ideas and experiences. Entertaining dialogue is a big part of any fun endeavor, whether hiking, sightseeing or dining out. If your partner is not in the same league as you from an intelligence standpoint (or vice versa) ask yourself – Will this interfere with our ability to grow and continue communicating together as the relationship matures? (Smiles and hugs only go so far.)

Lastly, "Married couples who have attained higher levels of education are less likely to divorce than less-educated couples ..." ("Divorce Rate, Education Conversely Related; Protection Varies By Race, Study Shows", March 11, 2013 Huffingtonpost.com). Equally as beneficial, highly- educated couples are usually far more capable of financially supporting themselves and others (namely your children) than less-educated couples. If your partner did not attend college or a trade school, think twice about marrying them.

**Marital Status -** Marrying a divorcee has its downsides. You may only be able to count on a small portion of their income to fund your household needs. A sizable percentage of what they earn might have to go to their ex in the form of alimony. And, if they have children living under another roof, additional mandatory support payments may be in order and some of your cash may be needed to assist with shortfalls. If this assistance harms your retirement savings or your ability to fund your own biological children's college education, how would you feel? More inclined to take your frustrations out on your spouse?

Aside from potentially having less disposable income on hand by marrying a previously divorced spouse, you may have to cope with less of their time and attention as well. Your step kids will rightfully require some of your spouse's undivided focus (yours as well), taking time away from you and your prodigy. And, your payback – Your step kids may never accept you the way you want to be accepted and doling out tough love (as if they were your own) may cause additional marital strains.

Previously married spouses are more likely to split up again than their "never-before-married" counterparts and the degree of risk increases for each subsequent marriage. (Those divorced once or twice are more likely to fail in their second or third marriages than someone getting married for their first time.) The U.S. Bureau of the Census in 2006 measured this increased risk to be in the double digit percentages. "People marrying today have a 50% chance of divorcing. *Statistically, 40% of first marriages, 60% of second, and 73% of third marriages end in divorce.*" (See

"Marriage, Family, & Stepfamily Statistics", Updated March 2013, by Ron L. Deal, at www.smartstepfamilies.com/view/statistics)

Final consideration to weigh: If your partner's parents have divorced, your partner may be more inclined to proceed down the same path. ("**Up to twice as likely**"according to research conducted by Nicholas H. Wolfinger, assistant professor at the University of Utah's Department of Family and Consumer Studies. See "Children of Divorced Parents Are More Likely to End Their Own Marriages", June 28, 2005, Ann Bardsley at www.medicalnewstoday.com)

**Political/Social Views** – If your partner is a fervent liberal Democrat and you an ardent conservative Republican, you will be in for an unpleasant surprise. Being on opposite sides of the fence when it comes to supporting (or not supporting) hotly contested social policies (i.e., on abortion, redistribution of wealth, healthcare reform, immigration policy, balanced budgets and gun control, to name a few), may cause tensions to escalate and spill over into your everyday life.

And, with Presidential election campaigns seemingly starting mid-term these days and so many offices to fill at the Federal, State and Local levels, there are numerous opportunities throughout the year for political conflict with your spouse. Each election period, regardless of whom you are casting your votes for (i.e., President, Governor or Town Councilman) you will effectively cancel each other out at the polls. For some this is a non-event. For others, a not so subtle reminder their spouse is not always on the same team and an adversary of sorts.

**Overall Health** – Ideally, you should marry someone who is roughly your own age, physically fit, emotionally well-adjusted and not genetically predisposed to major illness. Disease takes its toll on *both* spouses, sometimes more heavily on the one who becomes caregiver, and may be inherited by your unsuspecting offspring.

Simply put – Your spouse's health issues become your health issues and vice versa. If there is a large disparity between your physical and mental well-being and your partner's, your relationship will suffer. Every disease, whether it be a permanent debilitating variety (type I diabetes, congestive heart failure or bipolar depression) or a more manageable one (high blood pressure, chronic fatigue syndrome or a reproductive disorder) produces undesirable symptoms or side effects that will negatively impact both of you.

If you are unable to have children together, share in enjoyable common activities or maintain a somewhat normal functioning household due to disease or disability – Extra stress will be placed on your shoulders. Sure there is a way to lessen this load (i.e., adopt children, find a travel buddy or hire out help). However, a certain portion of this extra stress will always remain. What if you can't live on one salary? What if you are consistently held back by your spouse's low energy levels? (They need 10 hours of sleep a night and their "MOJO" doesn't kick in until the early afternoon.) Or, their high anxiety or OCD makes them too frenetic and controlling and you can't sleep in on the weekends?

Although you can't fully predict your partner's future health status - Why burden yourself with their pre-existing infirmities right out of the gate, *unless* you are well positioned to deal with them? On a similar note: Marrying someone much older and far more established than you may be appealing, but will that still be the case when they reach their golden years and you are still in your prime?

**Debt levels** – Your future spouse's credit card debt becomes **your** debt upon marriage, as does their ability to rack up additional IOUs. Shouldn't you inquire about this sooner rather than later during the dating process?

Also, consider other forms of debt your partner may be on the hook for. How will their college loans, in addition to yours, be paid off when you tie the knot? If they have home-mortgage-sized higher education borrowings and are not intending to work when you have kids, you need to discuss this in detail and address in writing. (More on prenuptial agreements below.) Starting a marriage off in a big financial hole is emotionally taxing. Devise a clear plan up front to tackle your debt load and specify how things should unfold in the event of divorce.

Should you have to continue paying off their pre-marital debt if they terminate the relationship? And, what if your families have been assisting with zero or low interest rate loans? We should all make good on **our** promises. But, should you have to continue doing the same for the promises of others when your marriage has officially ended?

In summary, the saying "opposites attract" might bring two people together, but it has no bearing on whether or not a relationship will last. The more differences you and your partner have, the less compatible you'll be and the more friction you will experience along the way. Don't marry thinking you can change your partner, so they think or act more like you or become more to your liking in certain areas. For the most part, people can't be changed.

If you love someone very much, have a lot in common with them and have weathered past storms together (passed the "stress test" as discussed next) don't pass up on them because they are from a poor family, less attractive than you (beauty radiates from the inside out) or of a different race, for instance. No one is a perfect match on negotiable commonalities! But if you can't trust them, they don't respect a dollar, or are lazy- cut your losses early. It is only a matter of time before your relationship fails.

## E. Stress - The Best Compatibility Test

You don't know someone's true colors until they experience adversity. Stress is like a truth serum. It's not easy hiding behind deceptively fake words and actions "when all hell breaks loose". The mental and physical discomfort associated with major stress-producing events oftentimes reveals who a person really is ... right down to their core beliefs and personality.

The loss of a job, interacting with difficult future in-laws, or even planning a formal celebration (i.e., engagement or wedding party) can be a blessing in disguise when dating. Think of the occurrence of these stress triggers as an opportunity to conduct a "dry run" for your future marriage. Should the results surprise, you can adjust accordingly.

Some major stress producing events to analyze closely when courting:

- *Disagreements with Future in-Laws* - If your partner has arguments with or about your parents or a sibling, take a step back and think through the why of it all. Is it always about the same topic? (I.e., Money, control or insecurities.) Are their arguments founded or unfounded? How likely will these same issues continue on into the marriage, harming it in the process?

    Even if your partner's reasoning for being disagreeable is sound - Do their reactions/punishment fit the crime? Are they capable of giving you and your loved ones the benefit of the doubt when things don't go as planned? Do they negatively interact with their own parents and other family members the same way as yours? How do these disagreements make you feel? Controlling tendencies only become more amplified in marriage. Carefully consider your ability to deal with them now rather than later.

- *Discord with Anything Engagement Related* – What if your future spouse insists on a more expensive engagement present than you think is appropriate or can afford? Or wants your parents to pay for a lavish engagement celebration in some faraway place? Or, their requests are reasonable monetarily, but the stress of coordinating it all (from formal announcements/invitations to party favors) is resulting in numerous heated quarrels in what should be routine matters? Then it would be perfectly acceptable to question – Are they the right partner for you? And, if the engagement is not going well, what makes you think your wedding and impending marriage will?

    Life is a continuum of stressful events from new and on-going challenges. How you, as a couple, deal with these challenges is a telling indicator of compatibility and ability to ride out tough times together. A controlling, "type

A", perfectionist, may be a great person, just not paired with another person possessing the same traits.

When evaluating stressful events - Focus on actions as well as words. Your future partner may vehemently state they believe in adhering to a budget, but receiving an expensive diamond studded wedding ring is a necessary one time exception to accurately measure your love or test your long term commitment level. Shouldn't a "keeper" understand a much better use of your money (their future money) would be to purchase a smaller, less costly ring and deposit the rest into an emergency fund or down payment on a home? Why go crazy purchasing a showcase ring that will be seldom used after a few years of marriage when kids and practicality reign the day. And, a more modest ring means you don't have to worry as much about it being lost or stolen.

- *Wedding Planning Strife* – Can't be eliminated in its entirety. Expect some level of discomfort. Your partner may have been planning their big day, to varying degrees, since early childhood. If they are looking to host a picture perfect ceremony on some remote tropical island, complete with lavishly adorned tents and other props - watch out! You may be in for a bumpy ride. But some understanding is in order. What might you be initially inclined to ask for if you had been dreaming about your ideal ceremony for more than a decade? Coming up with something extraordinary and emotionally charged might not be so out of the norm.

Regardless of hopes and aspirations, a wedding should conform to reality from a budgeting standpoint. If your future spouse demands: 1.A more expensive wedding than you can afford, 2. A lavish honeymoon that will put you in debt, or 3. Wedding attire fit for royalty ... You should again ask - Is this the right person for you? It's ok to splurge on certain items (i.e., fancy limo, live band or Viennese dessert bar) as long as you cut back in other areas so the total bill is manageable. Why go into debt for years, for a one day only event?

And, resist the temptation to accept money from anyone to fund your wedding. The acceptance of money will likely result in acceding control in such matters as: Where and when the wedding takes place, who sits near whom and how many guests your family gets to invite. **Pay for your own wedding!** There is no such thing as a "free lunch", even from relatives. Failure to do so can result in marital trouble for years down the road. That is, if you even get married in the first place. Take charge of your own destiny and live within (preferably below) your means in all aspects of life, including purchasing wedding services. If you can't afford a small, modest wedding, there is nothing wrong with eloping.

- *Job Loss and Resulting Money Trouble* – How someone responds to losing their job, speaks volumes about their character and work ethic. Are they resilient enough to get back in the game by applying for new work within a reasonable time period? Are they putting in full days searching for new work opportunities or only half-heartedly attempting to find something? Are they contemplating a career change during the transition period? If so, does it make sense to you? Do you get the impression your significant other would rather not work at all? If so, is that acceptable based on past discussions?

  Although the job market may be tough and positive results hard to come by – Their actions say a lot about who they are, especially if they are behind on school loans and car payments. Are they doing enough to help their own cause or are they expecting you to bail them out with little effort on their end? There is nothing wrong with assisting your fiancée/fiancé when they are doing everything within their own power to succeed. You are in it together and when you eventually get married, what's yours is theirs and vice versa, unless a prenuptial agreement is called for (see next section). If you can't envision your future spouse as a suitable business partner (your other half in a mission critical joint venture), take time to reflect on why?

## F. Prenuptial Agreements – Do You Need One?

*Disclaimer: This section is not intended to serve as a substitute for obtaining sound legal advice from a licensed attorney specializing in this subject in your state, territory or jurisdiction. My goal is simply to introduce you to an important concept using my limited knowledge of NJ law to shape the discussion.*

For starters - A prenuptial agreement (also known as a premarital or ante-nuptial agreement) is a contract signed by two consenting adults **before** they get married spelling out how **financial** assets will be distributed in the event of divorce. Although merely broaching this topic may harm your romance, it is a stress test/risk worth taking early on in a serious relationship if any of the conditions listed under the **"When Prenuptials are Critical"** section are applicable to you.

Note: A discussion about prenuptials shouldn't be perceived as a negative event. It can be a mutually beneficial exercise that gets you and your partner talking about a difficult, yet important topic. Engaging in this type of discussion doesn't mean you don't trust your partner. It signifies you care enough about your relationship to proactively take measures to minimize potential future conflict and legal/mediation costs (for them as well) in case things don't work out ... And, that it is more of a protective insurance policy that won't be needed if all goes well with the marriage.

If you don't see "eye-to-eye" before marriage on how things should be divided if you ever became legally separated (especially around the personal emotional "stuff" like family heirlooms and other valuable keepsakes *you* accumulated pre-marriage), cut your losses early. You want a partner who will marry you for who you are - Not for your money or possessions.

## Major Benefits
Besides further aiding in evaluating financial compatibility (and perhaps genuine love), a prenuptial agreement gives you more control over the divorce process. Why let a court of law solely deem what's fair in terms of an equitable split of wealth when you can have a say? [As of the time of this writing - without a prenuptial in place in non-commonwealth states like NJ, you may not receive half of your marital property in divorce, even though you may have contributed more than half.] In addition to defining property rights and distribution, a solid prenuptial can limit alimony payments in some cases. If your spouse cheats on you (adultery), you can stipulate to their forfeiture of certain assets. Although you may not be able to eliminate the heartache associated with divorce, you can at least minimize the financial sting (reduced or no alimony) with a little forethought.

All in all, entering into a prenuptial agreement will educate you about the legal implications of marriage, serve as a smart financial planning tool and act as a divorce insurance policy of sorts. A large percentage of marriages end in divorce. Nearly half by most accounts. Why not plan for the worst as you would by procuring homeowner's or car insurance policies? You have a greater chance of getting divorced than losing your house to fire or your car to theft.

## When Prenuptials are Critical
If you are on the fence about a prenuptial agreement and ***any*** of the below 7 conditions apply to you – It is highly recommended you enter into one to preserve your wealth (existing/future) and sanity:

- You make ***much more***  money than your partner or have accumulated substantially more assets than them. (I.e., you already own a home, large stock portfolio or valuable collection of something.)
- You have the prospect of making ***much more*** money than your spouse. For instance, you have a lucrative degree, such as an MD, JD or MBA from a top tier school.

- You already own a successful business. Nothing like giving away half the equity in your enterprise to someone who did not assume any of the initial risk and may have no intention of contributing to its ongoing profitability post-divorce.
- You may be receiving a *large* inheritance. You don't want someone marrying you for what your parents earned or accumulated over their lifetime.
- You have agreed to fund your future spouse's schooling. Some folks are opportunistic. They may use you to get what they want, but can't afford on their own, such as an advanced degree.
- Your partner will be entering marriage with *major* debt, perhaps school loans, you don't want to be on the hook for if things don't work out.
- You have kids from a prior marriage and want to ensure they are treated fairly.

## Important Considerations

As a first step, you and your partner should jointly create a rough draft prenuptial agreement, complete with contested provisions. (Not important you agree to everything at this stage.) This will save on legal fees and allow for more productive dialogue later on when you both meet with **separate** attorneys.

Yes, you need two attorneys. One attorney can't effectively serve both of your best interests. What if a conflict arises? Plus, it is unethical for an attorney to represent the two of you in this type of matter and could void the agreement as coerced.

Resist the temptation to consummate the prenuptial on your own without competent legal assistance by seeking the counsel of a skilled lawyer. In New Jersey, for example, at the time of this publication, **all** of the following bulleted conditions must be met to create a valid binding agreement:

- *Voluntarily executed* - Meaning no coercion by you or your partner and it must be signed before a neutral notary public. To reduce the risk or perception of coercion, sign the agreement well in advance of marriage, preferably before you are engaged.
- *Contains FULL disclosure of all assets* – If you are hiding assets and this is later discovered, the entire contract can be voided. If you can't be transparent about everything at this stage of your relationship (not talking about your first few dates), when will you ever be?
- *Fair to both parties* – If it contains unconscionable provisions or wacky demands, a judge may ignore the other reasonable ones. Stipulating that a divorce should result in one of you never seeing your kids again is one such example. Nor can you leave someone destitute regardless of fault.

Another consideration for creating an enforceable prenuptial agreement – Don't put **personal** responsibilities in the document. It should be all about money or assets that can be converted to money. If you include expectations around the division of household chores, who should hold a job (full time or part time) and how many kids to have - It increases the likelihood the entire document will be deemed invalid ... Meaning a court could strike down all of its provisions, including the reasonable ones.

A prenuptial agreement may not be bullet proof or the final word on who gets what, but it is a powerful tool nonetheless when properly drafted and executed to mitigate financial risk. Have a matrimonial and family law specialist, not a general practice attorney, aid you in the process. If you include unenforceable terms, such as those attempting to define child custody and child support, you may be doing more harm than good. (General practitioners may overlook this fact.)

In summary, enter into a prenuptial agreement when certain conditions apply to safeguard your assets. (Consult competent legal counsel to assist with the decision.) Your future spouse may be secretly adhering to the mantra "I can marry more money in a minute than I can earn in a lifetime." Prepare for the worst, expect the best.

## G. Relationship *"Saving"* Pointers

- **Gifting your services** - Instead of cash or traditional store bought items, gifting services is a cost effective way to let friends, family and significant others know you care about them. Marking special milestones, holidays and events (birthdays, anniversaries, Christmas, Mother's Day, etc.) with *free* babysitting, house cleaning or car waxing services, for example, will be much appreciated and requires little more than your time, loving attention and some "elbow grease". Be creative when generating ideas. There are countless ways to gift generously without having to dig deep into your pockets. If you are handy – How about offering your lawn maintenance, gutter cleaning or painting expertise? Or, giving a full body massage to your "better half" if preparing a romantic home-cooked meal is not your thing? And, nothing compliments a gifted service better than a handmade card with a sincere personalized message.
- **No business with friends or family** – Some degree of separation is healthy in any close relationship and nothing more ruinous than disagreements over money. If teaming up with your brother, brother-in-law, best friend or spouse to pursue a dream business sounds like an excellent idea – Think twice about it! Small businesses are risky (the majority fail within the first five years) and usually require you to be joined at the hip with your partner(s) to make it

succeed ... Meaning putting in long hours together, week in and week out, sometimes 24/7, under stressful situations all in the name of turning a decent profit. And, even if you are lucky to land a "silent" partner (they just supply the financing while you run the day to day operations), they are not so silent when their return on investment fails to excite. Good friends are hard to find and family tends to treat fellow family the harshest (lack of filters). Why damage solid relationships over money?

- **Importance of a unified savings approach** - Keeping separate bank accounts and only sharing the payment of common bills can undermine your marital relationship by creating an environment lacking in trust and discipline. What incentive does your partner have to optimize savings when all they have to set aside each month is 50% of the mortgage/property taxes, utilities and food expenses? In other words, why should your partner work extra hard saving a buck when what you save on your side will most likely benefit them anyway? A marriage requires an "all hands on deck" approach and both partners should have a say in the overall marital savings rate. If your savings rate is high and your spouse's is low to nonexistent – what are you accomplishing?

- **Encourage your prospective marriage partner to read this guide** - Or others like it, such as *The Millionaire Next Door: The Surprising Secrets of America's Wealthy* (1996, by Thomas J. Stanley). By soliciting their opinions and gauging reactions, you should be able to tell if you are compatible from a monetary perspective. If you sense your potential future fiancée/fiancé is into status, can't make financial sacrifices, or sees nothing wrong with spending future income (carrying debt) - you should look elsewhere for a marriage partner even if they generate an impressive income. Again, what good is making big bucks if they can't spend much less than they earn? (One of the pillars of creating wealth.) Be on the lookout for partners who say they agree with things, but their body language, tone and or actions/inactions (i.e., pretend to read something without giving it serious consideration) say differently. Love may spur someone to lie to hold onto it, especially if they sense you might go in another direction with the relationship.

- **Teaching your children who to marry** - Is as critical to their happiness and financial well-being as yours. Your future children's failure is in many ways your failure. If your kids marry someone who bankrupts them (could be post-divorce), you will come to their emotional and financial aid. And if grandchildren are involved, your assistance might be substantial. (So much so, your retirement savings could be negatively impacted.) Although there are no guarantees in life, especially when it comes to marriage – Educating your children from a young age on what to look for in a mate (desirable traits, values and habits) is an important step in mitigating their divorce risk. And, it works both ways. A marriage can be broken if your son or daughter can't hold a job, because they are lazy, still finding themselves, or not a desirable job candidate. (More on this topic in the next chapter.)

In review, your relationships have a larger financial impact on your net worth than you may imagine. Picking the right marriage partner, for instance, is a high stakes game. A poor choice could harm your financial well-being and that of your future children for a long time. One key factor to take into consideration before walking down the aisle - Are you, yourself, currently commitment worthy? If not, hold off until you are ready with the understanding that everyone matures at different rates and some folks may never be ready for all that a marriage entails. (It is perfectly fine if, for the right reasons, you don't ever get married.)

There is a significant emotional and dollar cost associated with divorce. Therefore, don't jump the gun and make a deliberate effort to: 1) Fully explore that you and your loved one are an excellent match from a key commonality standpoint, 2) Carefully analyze whether or not you pass the courtship/dating "stress test" (future stress can be even more intense when more is at stake); 3) Set the right expectations well in advance of marriage to protect yourself via a mutually entered into prenuptial agreement when called for. Your destiny, in large part, is held in who you marry - and can make for either a very easy or very difficult life.

# CHAPTER 9

## Children

*If your future kids are not armed with successful savings techniques by the time they graduate college (a critical time to landing on their own two feet), your retirement savings/nest egg and all that you have worked so hard for, will be under attack.*

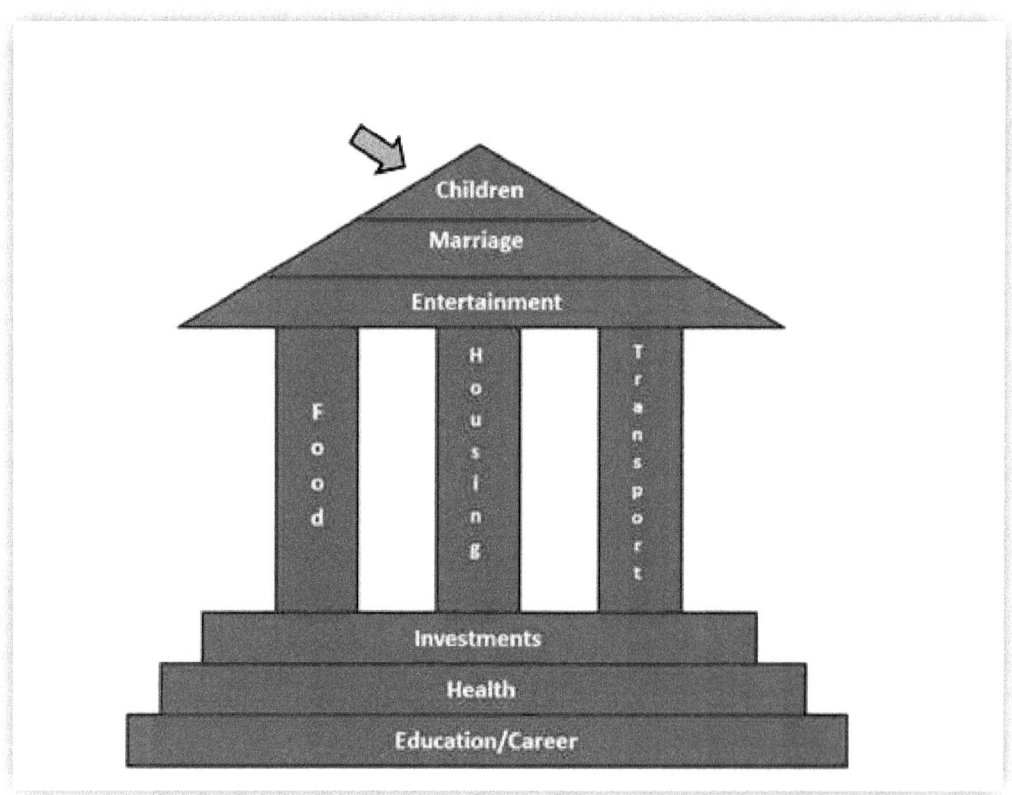

Building & maintaining EFI by managing your "spend"/focus on your children.

## A. Overview

Although having children is probably the furthest thing from your mind right now (hopefully it is if you are still in school), exposing yourself to the concepts in this final chapter at an early age should enable you to better relate to your parents and in turn, spend more quality time focusing on building your "dream home" – an advantage in your quest to attain and retain EFI

Your children's savings success has a direct impact on your future financial independence. The less they are able to care for themselves as young adults, the more assistance they will seek from you, including monetary support. And, bigger kids, mean bigger problems. "Do you have spare change for a pack of gum?" in elementary school becomes "Can you help with my apartment rent?" post college.

Children grow up fast and you can't re-coup impressionable lost time. Introduce them as early as practical to the principles in this guide so they can fully function on their own when you "cut the cord" and they become emancipated. Your most important role as a parent is to raise **independent** children that don't need you someday.

You won't be around forever to care for them. Even if you are fortunate to live well into your eighties or nineties, temporarily postponing the inevitable – Declining health and dwindling income/principal will most likely render you unable to care for anyone but yourself by then. **Tough love** is the best way to ensure your kids become self-sufficient. And, they don't call it "tough" love for nothing. There will be many trying parent/child experiences along the way to setting them free that will be worth enduring in the end.

Tough love builds character and strength out of adversity and failure if you successfully avoid falling into the following parental pitfalls: **1)** ***Doing everything for your kids*** (aka enabling). It softens them and gets in the way of accomplishing your main mission. Learn to gradually let go as they become more proficient at taking care of themselves in matters. **2)** ***Refraining from doling out discipline***, because you are overly concerned about being cool or well-liked by your children. Being their best friend is not in your parental job description ... Nor is overcompensating for feelings of guilt attributable to one or more of your parental short comings. We all make mistakes – Learn to live with them and move on. **3)** ***Expecting anyone other than you and your spouse to teach your kids the value of money and related EFI concepts***. It's your responsibility, not that of higher education or any other institution for that matter. College may do an impressive job helping students find themselves, learn from failure and test their outer limits ... all within its relatively safe confines before the harsh realities of the real world surface. However, Academia will not teach your children many things, including how to successfully manage their personal finances, while making smart money decisions along the way.

As you read the rest of this chapter, please keep in mind - Tough love really works. Instead of shielding your children from failure, let them "strike out" on their own. Failing early and often builds confidence as they learn from their mistakes. Instead of swinging unsuccessfully at the next "curveball" life has in store for them, they will eventually adjust waiting for their sweet spot. Perhaps an outside fastball they can hit out-of-the-park like they did countless times before in the sanctuary of your backyard *after* you personally showed them how with their own little bat. Leading by example is the best instructional aid and motivator you have at your disposal. What little kid doesn't want to be more like their parents? Walk the talk and you'll have a follower.

## B. Avoid "Enabling" – In the Negative Sense of the Word

What is enabling? Although the term has a positive side, it is most frequently used to refer to negative, harmful interactions with others. "Any time you assist/allow another person to continue in their unproductive/unhealthy/addictive behavior, whether actively or passively, you are enabling ...Sometimes enabling takes the form of doing something for another that they should do for themselves."(Darlene Albury, LCSW at www.asktheinternettherapist.com).

Make no mistake about it - This concept relates to your future children! **Don't do for your kids what they should be doing on their own**. In other words, teach them how to fish then step aside. If you always put fish on their plate, how will they ever learn to hone their own casting techniques? What message does this send? That others will always be around to lend a helping hand? That they are entitled to assistance?

At no time is enforcing the "do not enable" rule more important than when your children reach young adulthood. Therefore, avoid the temptation to enable your adult children to create a life that's unsustainable without your assistance. Providing them with unearned money, unreasonable emotional support and/or basic services they should be providing for themselves (i.e., doing their own cooking, laundry, housekeeping, landscaping, shopping, childrearing, etc.) does them more harm than good.

By making it possible for your children to avoid the negative consequences of their actions, they will fail to learn from their failures. Propping them up or sheltering them from life's realities inevitably leads to a false sense of accomplishment and security, turning their weaknesses into debilitating sores and sadly encouraging poor decision making with undesirable outcomes.

As an extreme, but not too far-fetched example: What if your future son is not ready for marriage and you "buy" him a spouse, complete with a fully furnished home, and play the role of surrogate husband/handyman for his wife? No matter how much you may desire grandkids, you are doing him and others a disservice. If he's not ready for children and starts down that path, you may feel compelled to further assist by providing childcare services or money to "keep the peace" (his marital harmony). However, what happens when a second or third child arrives, your son is no more well-adjusted than before, and you become emotionally, physically and financially tapped out?

Your daughter-in-law may counter with an "easy come, easy go" approach. Essentially, walking away from everything because she can't respect her husband (no matter how much money and support you provide), unraveling what you unnaturally created and sustained. And, this scenario could take a turn for the worse. What if you and your spouse pass away and are unavailable to assist your son (weakened by your past meddling) with picking up the "broken pieces" left behind by a messy divorce? Don't mistakenly believe your child's siblings, cousins, aunts or uncles will carry on where you left off. They have their own lives, wives, kids and or grandkids to focus on. Besides, if you didn't raise a man (or self-sufficient woman), what makes you think they can?

Money doesn't solve everything! Throwing cold cash at your children, pre or posthumous, only goes so far. It doesn't compensate for failing to teach them to be independent and street smart, without which they can be swindled out of everything or make extremely poor financial decisions resulting in the same effect. And, all the money in the world can't raise healthy, well adjusted, loving offspring. Even if you can afford to provide your children with the 24/7 services of an entire community (i.e., personal tutors, advisors and mental health therapists), your role doesn't change. You can't buy a substitute parent. It is your responsibility, and your responsibility alone, to fill those big shoes. Hold yourself accountable, and do your part.

In summary: Don't be an enabler. The best love is tough love and this entails holding back various types of support when appropriate even when you are feeling guilty about not having done enough as a parent! Money isn't a cure all.

## C. Their Failure is Your Failure?

Only if you allow it! Or, "can't let go", thereby preventing your children from learning for themselves through trial and error. As a parent you can't help but feel empathy for them when they fail at something - you hurt when they hurt. [But take comfort in knowing: They won't grow unless they experience varying degrees of discomfort and pain by "experimenting" outside their comfort zone.] We live vicariously through our children, an extension of ourselves, and want the very best for them. Therefore, their burdens naturally become our burdens.

However, this does not equate to "their failures are our failures". You are *partially* responsible for your children's ability or inability to succeed in this world, especially from a savings and EFI perspective. You can't stand in their place to take their academic tests, defend their team's goal or invite their secret "crush" to the big dance so the results are successful and heartbreak is averted. But, you can train yourself when to best refrain from providing hands-on assistance, remaining on the side-lines instead as a spirited coach, mentor and spectator. How else will your children learn to be **accountable** for their actions? (More on accountability shortly.) If you write their book report (because they waited until the last minute, just don't get it, or are exhibiting signs of laziness) – does this better position them to write their own next time around?

You owe it to yourself to invest significant time raising your children from day one. If you wait until they reach a certain age or grade in school to turn up the heat, you might be too late. Why not start as soon as they are capable of processing what needs to be conveyed? Remember - Your children's burdens will be your burdens someday. And, ironically their material/financial needs reach their peak when you are least able to gamble with your savings. After assisting your children with college and perhaps graduate school expenses, you will likely be in your 50's or early 60's with limited time remaining to fund your retirement accounts.

The last thing you need to deal with (with limited working time left in your career) is a struggling young adult child who needs major assistance paying basic living expenses, like rent, utilities or food. You may be able to sit idly by, exerting tough love when your child is floundering in a dead end minimum wage job. However, will you be able to let them pay for their mistakes when innocent grandkids are involved? If your kids mess up badly enough you will come to their rescue.

Your main parental mission should be raising well adjusted, level headed, financially savvy kids that can make it on their own someday and train their own kids to do the same. If they can't fly (leave your nest) when you are ready to retire, your whole way of life will be under siege from the additional weight of their shortcomings or failures. And, if you are not consistent, staying the course with each and every child, the results will be the same. You can't let up on your second or third child, because you are overwhelmed or forced into making difficult compromises. Subsequent children shouldn't be burdened by your decisions. You owe it to them. They did not ask to be born.

## D. Invest in Your Children's Success

The best way to do so, aside from reviewing the previous sections of this savings guide with them, is to teach **Accountability** (a form of discipline or punishment). In other words, hold them liable, responsible or answerable for their actions/inactions early on in life. If they don't do the right things (completing homework, achieving good grades or performing essential household chores), let them pay the price for their mistakes.

Your children will likely learn from their missteps and become better off for it. (I.e., Improved grades, stronger skill sets and enhanced character.)

If you don't hold your children 100% accountable for their actions – What kind of message are you sending? If you give them money earmarked for a particular use and they spend *all* of it on other things – They should have to live with their decisions, even if it means doing without for a long period of time. Teaching your children the value of properly managing money *at an early age* is critical. However, not as critical as having them answer for all their actions from day one in a way that may very well re-shape their future behavior, setting the table for repeatable success.

Giving your children the gift of accountability extends to matters well beyond budgeting, school work and chores. If your child is involved in a car accident, no matter how minor, they should own up to it. If they get caught fleeing an accident scene, for example, and receive a citation from law enforcement - don't help them fight the charges. They should pay for their crime and then perhaps next time they will do the right thing (stop and exchange insurance, license and registration information) so their mistake can be properly be dealt with.

Other ways to invest in your children's success, consider teaching or grooming them to exhibit the following traits to increase their chances of attaining and maintaining EFI:

- **Independence** - Prepare your kids to live on their own, while they are still under your roof, so they can function well without you as soon as practical upon graduating from college. Living on their own (a form of independence) will refine their budgeting skills and reinforce the importance of pursuing a solid career. Note: An "empty nest" is healthy. Fight your feelings to continue nurturing your kids long after you should be. There is no such thing as perfect timing. If a mother bird waited for the right wind speed, temperature, humidity and lighting for her offspring to voluntarily leave the nest it might never happen. Therefore, when necessary, she coaxes or taunts them to leave to facilitate the process.
- **Spirituality** – A deep faith in a higher power or belief system provides something to fall back on during times of trouble and spurs us on to greatness when we are less than such. An important code of conduct I try my best to adhere to is living the Golden Rule. What does this require? Simply treating others as we wish to be treated. If you say people are important, but don't show through actions you really mean it – Your credibility will suffer and your goals/dreams may become delayed or unfulfilled. (What goes around, comes around … Meaning your harmful actions have inadvertent/advertent consequences.)

- **Generosity** - You don't want to raise the next Scrooge. If your children can't give to others, how well adjusted will they be with friends, business colleagues and spouses? Have your children donate a portion of their cash gifts to church, charities and other good causes. When money is tight, show them how to lend their time and energy to others in need. Assisting with the preparation of food for the homeless is one way to give back that is very gratifying.
- **Humbleness** – You shouldn't broadcast your every success to the world, including your close friends and neighbors. Nobody likes a braggart. And, most people, except your parents and grandparents, are not sincerely excited or happy for you when you do well and may even be jealous to some extent. Teach your kids to keep their stellar accomplishments close to the vest. Why upset anyone or create unnecessary rivalries/competitions? You are better served not wearing your successes on your sleeve for all to see so you are less of a target for the jealous.
- **Happiness** - Material things don't bring sustained happiness. And, to a certain extent, more of anything actually means less, as it distorts perceptions and results in under appreciation. If you buy your children everything they want, you will soften them. Ten pairs of sneakers, one in every color, will not make them any happier than owning just one quality pair. Instead of teaching your kids to be world class shoppers, show them how to have fun and laugh so they can better cope with stressful events.

**Importance of leading by example** – Advice alone is not going to help your kids if you don't demonstrate how it's applied. If you are not accountable, independent, spiritual, generous, humble or happy - What makes you think your kids will be? To foster true learning you must be a good role model and **lead by example!** "Walking the talk" is critical to reinforcing any advice.

In other words, what you do (your actions) is far more educational and likely to stick with your subjects than merely speaking about it conceptually. Words can be cheap, especially when actions contradict them. If you want your kids to be committed to attending church, but you yourself won't go (just drop them off at Sunday school) – What are you really saying? The same thing pertains to prayer. If you lecture on its importance, but you don't recite prayers with your children at bedtime or say grace before dinner, you are undermining the importance of your message.

Leading by example is the best way to teach your kids the value of money and to encourage them to save at an early age. If you say one thing (save), and do the other (spend recklessly) you will send mixed messages to your children and your actions, not your words, will resonate the most. Therefore, for the savings related principles outlined in this guide to last a lifetime and lead to another generation of monetary success - They must be backed up by *your* actions to become engrained in your children's every fiber. If you don't practice what you preach, why should your children?

## E. Saving without Sacrificing Quality or Safety

It takes big bucks to raise a child …by some accounts 250 to 500k, excluding the cost of a college education. (U.S. Department of Agriculture, on-line calculator using 2011 figures at http://www.cnpp.usda.gov/calculatorintro.htm.) And, the lifetime cost of raising a child is understandably more for middle-class income and above families living in major metropolitan areas. Families with higher disposable incomes tend to spend more on their children, because **they can** and those living in higher cost regions, because **they must**.

The annual cost of child-rearing for a married couple living in the Northeast is estimated to be approximately $27,000. (As of 2013, according to finance expert Eleanor K.H. Blayney) Before starting a family, ask yourself – Do you have enough savings to meet a newborn's needs for at least year one? Can you afford to live on one income if your spouse doesn't plan to return to work after maternity leave? Conversely, if they intend to return to work – Can you afford adequate daycare arrangements? If any answer is "No" – Postpone having children until you are comfortable saying "Yes".

When the time is right, save on child-related expenditures without sacrificing quality or safety by: (Some of these concepts were covered in Chapter 4. Food/Essentials, under the "7 Ways to Save" section, but are worth reviewing again in this context.)

- *Purchasing regularly consumed essentials in bulk* – When they are on sale of course. Purchasing nonperishables, such as diapers, way ahead of time in many different sizes is the way to go. If your child outgrows a particular size and the package is un-open, most retailers will allow you to exchange it for a larger size.
- *Paying a little more for items when it makes sense* - Price should not be the only factor influencing your purchase decisions. Premium diapers cost more upfront, but offer much better absorbency than off-brands, resulting in fewer leaks/accidents and soiled clothes to tend to. If you live in an apartment and rely on coin operated laundry equipment, less loads for your kid's clothes means more coinage in your pocket.
- *Opting for breast milk over formula* – Formula is expensive. The less you need, because you are relying on breast milk instead, the more you will be able to save and spend on other essential supplies. Additionally, breast feeding saves time (fewer bottles to clean and warm) and is healthier for babies than formula

according to several reputable sources, including The American Academy of Pediatrics.

- *Buying gently worn baby clothes* - Thrift stores, consignment shops and private sales (house, garage or church) often offer incredible buys on slightly used children's clothing and accessories. In the first year of life, your baby may only wear something one or two times before they outgrow it. Why purchase something brand new at a premium that will get so little use?
- *Hiring a private caregiver when you have two or more kids* - If both you and your spouse work and you have two or more pre-school aged children – Consider hiring a private in-home caregiver to watch them. This less costly than paying for multiple kids in daycare at the same time and more convenient. Plus, if you get to work from home on occasion, you'll be able to spend more time with your kids during permissible downtime, such as lunch.
- *Living in a "top town"* – Is synonymous with great school districts. Instead of living in a lesser tier town, where you may have to opt for private school for grades K through 12 (13 long years) - Put your higher property taxes to work to secure an excellent free public education and perhaps safer environment for your kids. Would you rather own a large house with a 10K tax bill in an average town, or a smaller one with a 15K base in a top town? How much private school can you buy with the tax delta? About half an academic year if you are lucky.
- *Heavily utilizing your local library* - Encourage your children to borrow books, movies and music from their local library instead of buying them. Why pay for something they will likely read/use only once, when it can be loaned out for free (or a nominal fee) without inconveniencing anyone else? Flexing to library books over private retail copies, for example, sends a powerful message about the importance of conserving, recycling and avoiding materialism.
- *Finding free things to do* - There are surprisingly a lot of "special" activities you can participate in without spending any money - From attending exhibits at local museums, science centers and historical places to frequenting educational, musical or cultural events sponsored by area libraries, churches and municipalities/counties. Free activities are often advertised online or in your local newspaper.
- *Cutting your kids hair* – Even if you are not much of a barber or stylist. When your kids are young, they don't need fancy haircuts. You can practically put a bowl over their head and cut around it to make them look respectable. Invest in a "clipper kit" and you'll be glad you did. With inexpensive kid's haircuts costing around $10.00 (without tip) as of the time of this writing, you'll break even on hair trimming equipment (electric shaver and scissors) in two or three cuts. And, you'll become more proficient with each passing attempt.

## F. Important but Unrelated Thoughts

- **Your children need role models other than you** – Kids have a tendency to discount their parent's advice and actions as I did myself when I was a minor living at home. I'm not sure of all the reasons why as I look back ... other than my parents were just being parents and couldn't always relate to the unique needs of a younger generation and vice versa on my behalf. Regardless of "why", your future kids will occasionally ignore or minimize your advice – Don't be discouraged. It doesn't mean you are not a good parent. You can offset their natural aversion to learning from you by pointing them in the direction of role models who share your core beliefs. When kids hear or see something from others they respect, whether it is a successful neighbor, sports coach or school teacher, it usually sinks in faster. Everyone benefits from having a mentor and your initially "overlooked" advice, when validated elsewhere, will be reinforced all the more. Do your best to encourage the formation of mentor/mentee life changing relationships.
- **Don't burden your children with your future care** – Unless your children are a huge success, they may not have enough money to support you and their own immediate families in the event you experience an emergency or crisis. With long term care facilities (nursing homes) in some regions of the country averaging $106,000 per year for a semi-private room and assisted living facilities around $68,000 annually, you could be one health scare away from losing your financial independence. (Genworth's 2012 Long Term Care Survey at http://www.genworth.com) That is unless you take out long-term care insurance when you get much closer to retirement to protect your assets and prevent the possibility of having your home transferred to someone else to pay for your care. Also consider purchasing life insurance and long-term disability policies, if you can afford them to preserve what you have worked so hard for, and so your kids don't feel compelled to support you through trying times.
- **Don't put the "roof" on first!** - In keeping with the theme of this guide, make sure your foundation (schooling/career) and frame (transportation/housing) are fully secured *before* having children. Introducing a newborn into this world while you are still in school, for instance, has a devastating impact on your ability to stabilize your finances and achieve EFI. It takes two well-anchored adults making decent money to properly raise a child. How can this be accomplished if you and your partner are still attending high school or college with a limited income stream? You may have to forgo graduating, or significantly delay the receipt of your diploma, further damaging your long-term financial prospects. Along these same lines, don't have children

outside of a healthy marriage. The effects can be similar to undergoing a stressful divorce, even if you eventually decide to tie the knot.

- **Consider having children by age 30** - As long as you are emotionally and financially ready. Having children earlier in life, rather than later, has significant benefits. You'll have more physical stamina to corral active toddlers and compete right alongside athletic teenagers. You'll also be more capable of burning the candle at both ends when it comes to work and family pursuits. And, some studies suggest having children while you are young enough (between the ages of 27 and 32) so they can be launched into the real world by the time you turn 50, contributes to *extra happiness* at least as it relates to women. ("Learn about relationships from the happiest woman" by Gail Sheehy http://yourlife.usatoday.com/parenting-family/new-passages/story/2011)
*Extra happiness* that could allow you to be even more effective at saving in your later stages and gearing up for a fruitful retirement era ... All because you will be free of care giving responsibilities at a "reasonable" age. Caution: You don't want to be too young of a parent (under 25 for most guys). If you have children too soon in life, it may negatively impact your ability to invest in yourself first. It's hard to give of yourself, if you have nothing in reserve from an emotional and monetary perspective.

- **Does providing an allowance send the right message?** – Paying your children to perform household chores isn't a bad idea per se. It teaches them the correlation between work and money, the importance of being responsible and what it's like to manage a personal budget. "No work, no money, no savings, no fun" is certainly a great educator regarding the realities of life. However, shouldn't your children have a moral prerogative to contribute around the house *without compensation* for the overall good of the family? And, from what I've experienced, forgoing an allowance promotes harmony, fosters early childhood independence and instills genuine confidence ... Besides side stepping the inevitable and unpleasant "I need a raise" conversations. Your children will only learn the true value of a dollar by working for others (i.e., odd jobs with neighbors), not when you as a parent shower them with money for doing what they should be doing any way to earn their keep. You can't effectively be both parent and work boss. A true boss can fire them. Can you?
- **Be honest with yourself about wanting children** – As you mature and settle into a successful career and lifestyle, you may discover children are not for you. If you are brutally honest in your self-assessment and can live with the long term consequences of your decision – The "Why" is immaterial! There is nothing worse than bringing an unwanted child into this world when you

as a parent are ill-equipped and or unwilling to properly care for them. Once you have them, you can't return them. They are yours forever and you are on the hook to raise them. Hence, the decision not to have children, in certain circumstances, is quite admirable.

Although I admittedly still have much to learn on the topic of being a successful parent (as I have yet to raise my boys to adulthood), I do know based on my own upbringing and the experiences of other parents the advice herein works. If you don't enable your children, let them learn from their failures and invest in their success by holding them accountable and leading by example – Your **"personal roof"** will do what a roof should do. It will protect and sustain you … by safeguarding against the loss of your hard earned EFI, as can also result from improperly managing your entertainment/service related expenditures and marrying an incompatible spouse.

# Summary:

Congratulations! By reading the preceding chapters, you have already taken your "first step" towards reaching Early Financial Independence (EFI) ... A wonderfully liberating place/state of existence where you can experience the great American Dream in a debt free manner at a relatively young age (30's and 40's), while still being able to enjoy life to its fullest.

Imagine the freedom and sense of relief you will someday feel when you own everything outright, including a comfortable home and reliable car, and don't have any major money worries on your mind? And, picture yourself being able to focus more on what matters most to you. Perhaps, your loved ones, additional leisure time and exciting travel adventures – all because you are not enslaved to banks, mortgage companies and creditors.

The good news: No matter how dire things become economically here in the United States and beyond, there will always be "winners". You too can join that elite group at or near the top, overcoming many obstacles along the way, if you want it bad enough. Your "journey of a thousand miles" to EFI (where you will be rewarded with your very own Personal Savings Success Shelter) is attainable if you adopt an attitude of no turning back! You have 20 or 30 years to intermittently crawl, walk and run those miles so the trip is not as daunting as it may seem. Rome was not built in a day and you too have ample time (if you don't squander it) to build lasting wealth from the ground up at an early age ... Starting with a solid personal foundation, sturdy frame and quality roof so you are someday sheltered from destructive storms and other damaging elements.

Your success ultimately hinges on your ability to perform *much better than average* in managing your "spend"/focus in **all** of the applicable key challenge areas presented along the path to EFI: **Education/Career, Health, Investments, Food/Essentials, Housing/Shelter, Transportation, Entertainment/Services, Marriage/Friends** and **Children.**

With a little bit of luck (we all need some in life), if you adhere to the following advice, you will be fine: Take you studies and choice of career seriously, especially when you are being supported by your parents. Take good care of your physical and emotional health so you can leverage your greatest asset (your mind & body) to make well informed investment decisions that at a minimum preserve your hard earned capital. When the time is right to buy your own necessities, don't bite off more home than you can chew and avoid letting your car drive you into the poor house. Many years from now, when you finally reach full maturity, you may want to get married and have children. If so, spend considerable time selecting a compatible spouse. Who you marry can make or break you. And, be sure to raise children who are accountable by doling out tough love and leading by example so they won't kick you in the wallet while you are transitioning to retirement.

Don't fret. Attaining and maintaining EFI does not mean you need to be *the very best* in each of the aforementioned areas. Just being a high performer in every category can equate to tremendous success. Year after year, for example, Larry Bird who formerly played for the Boston Celtics, ranked amongst the top NBA basketball players in scoring, rebounding, assists and free-throw shooting percentages. Except in the latter category, he was never #1 in any other important statistic, yet he was voted the league's best player (MVP) in three consecutive seasons. Why? He excelled at so many things, including leading by example, which motivated his fellow teammates to perform at a higher level, ultimately leading to three championships.

Although you may never make millions of dollars a year like a top athlete or win any elite trophies or awards in your field or profession, you can still earn a very decent salary if you excel in the right major and apply yourself on the job. It's not what you earn, but what you save that makes the biggest difference in achieving the underlying goal of this guide. (Savings alone can be the difference between a comfortable life and a stressful existence worrying about how you'll support yourself.) And, if you lead a healthy lifestyle, invest solidly in yourself (education and career) and make intelligent decisions around your expenditures and investments you should be in for a great "Bird" like ride assuming you select the right marriage partner and instill your values in your offspring.

You will no doubt experience setbacks along the way. That's just how it is. But remember, it's not how many times you fall that matters most - it's how many times you get back up. By repeatedly visualizing the end results of your success, you will find the extra motivation to continue on your journey and eventually arrive at your final destination (EFI) with the on-going assistance of certain essential character traits - **Patience**, **Persistence**, **Focus**, **Discipline** and **Action.**

Don't be afraid to pay your dues in the early years - missing out on fun in the name of sacrifice as you build your personal home/shelter from scratch. And, "resist the temptation to cut corners". No personal homebuilding stage is more important than the other. Each plays a critical role in protecting overall structural integrity. A completed home is more valuable than the sum of its parts when it comes to your financial protection and *living below your means* on a consistent basis is the only way to get there ... As is starting as early as possible with your savings plan, and exhibiting a solid work ethic in all you do.

Some say the long and arduous journey to the top is the most enjoyable aspect of living and that once you reach the peak and savor in the awe inspiring view – There is nowhere to go but down. That may be true with mountain climbing – But I can assure you, leading a zero debt life at an early age (EFI) is exhilarating and well worth the ongoing maintenance sacrifices if you can fully appreciate how far you have travelled and resist resting on your past laurels. There is a reason why "The ladder of success is never crowded at the top" (Napoleon Hill). Uncover those reasons for yourself and you'll be glad you did.

I don't pretend to have all the answers. And, none of my advice is new or ground breaking, just based on common sense and my own life experiences. You will inevitably hear (if you have not already) much of what I have said stated by other reputable sources, such as your parents, financial professionals and self-help gurus as you grow and expand your horizons. However, what makes this savings guide so unique is that it's holistic in nature (multi-dimensional) and comes with a tried and true blueprint to follow that is two generations in the making.

If it can work for me, it can work for you. The choice is yours. You can continue following my proven game plan for savings success, modify it to meet your unique needs or do nothing (almost sure failure). Which one is it going to be so you too can experience the wonderful benefits of being financially free in the prime of your life and beyond?

# Appendix A

## Explanatory Drawing of Your Personal Savings Success Shelter

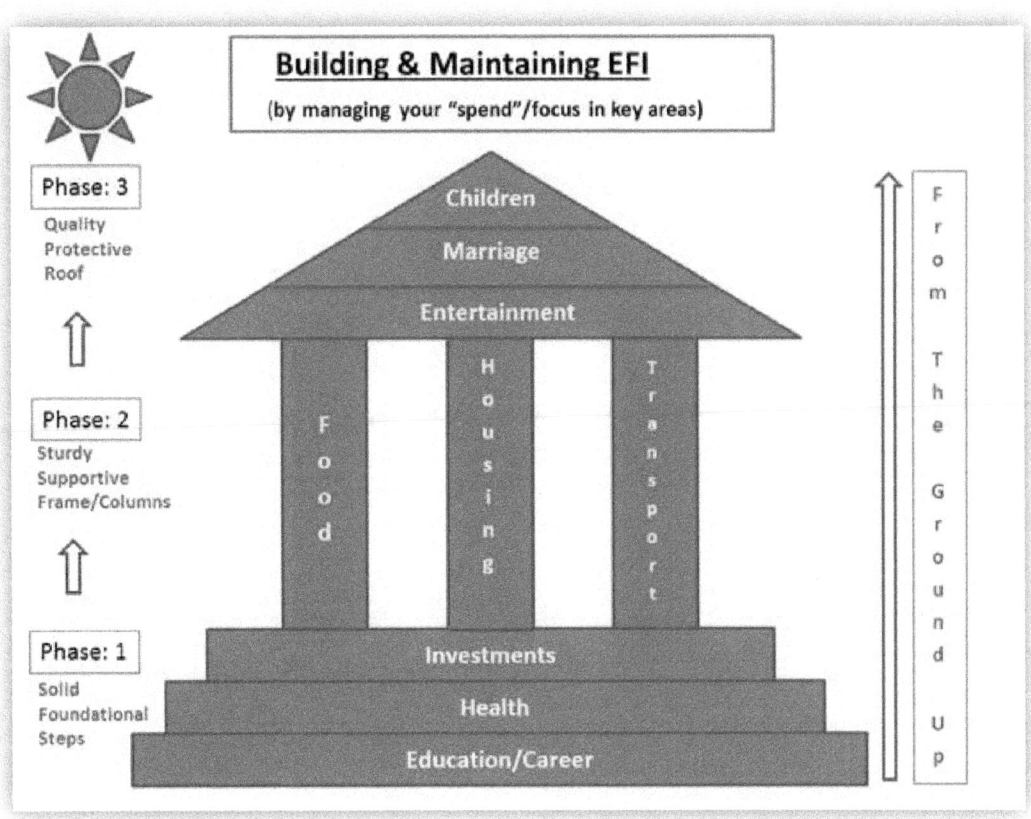

# Appendix B

**Sample Monthly Personal Income Statement**

| **Column A** <br> *(Revenue/Income/Profits)* | **Column B** <br> *(Expenses/Liabilities/Losses)* |
|---|---|
| Wages/Net Pay | Car Loans/Maintenance/Repairs/Fuel |
| Interest Income | Mortgage Payment |
| (Savings accts/CD's/Bonds) | Property Taxes |
| Dividends | Insurance (Car, home; health/medical) |
| (From Stocks and Funds) | Utilities (Gas, Electric; Water) |
| Savings Account Balance | Food |
| Checking Account Balance | Child Care (Daycare/aftercare/camp) |
| Money Market Balance | Personal Care (Clothes, haircuts) |
| Certificate of Deposit Balance | Continuing Education |
| Value of Mutual Funds/Stock Portfolio and Individual Stock Holdings | Entertainment/Vacations |
| | Charity/Gifts |
| Rental Property Income | Commuting expenses/tolls/train/parking |
| Royalties from Patents | Dry cleaning |
| Assets* (Car, home(s), furniture, etc.) | Student Loans/Credit card debt |
| | Miscellaneous/Unexpected repairs |
| Total: "X" | Total: "Y" |

If **Column A - B** (**"X" – "Y"**) **= a positive number** – Congratulations!! You are operating in the ***Black***. Meaning you are living within or below your means and saving money (Experiencing a temporary profit).

If **Column A – B = a negative number** - You are operating in the ***Red***. Meaning you are living beyond your means and not saving any money (Experiencing a loss).

*Assets don't produce revenue, income or profits until sold. Only list those you are absolutely willing to liquidate to cover additional expenses, liabilities or losses ... Or, to reduce existing ones. And, be conservative in your valuation.

# About the Author

Todd Manning, a happily married middle-aged father of two young boys, currently resides with his family in Westfield, New Jersey … The same affluent, suburban town he was raised in as a teenager and where he has been a proud homeowner since 1999.

A licensed Attorney and corporate software sales consultant for most of his career, Todd is married to an Ivy League educated Chemical Engineer (with a Masters in Engineering) who has worked for the pharmaceutical industry in various capacities since graduating from college. Despite living in one of the most expensive states in the nation, and graduating from law school with zero savings in 1993, he and his wife Caroline still managed to achieve financial freedom at the ages of 41 and 35 respectively and rank Top 5% or higher in U.S. household/family income and net worth.

He and Caroline own their upper-middle class home outright today (mortgage free since 2008). And, the same can be said of their cars and other possessions … Due in large part to their own efforts (no inheritance or other family assistance beyond their parents so graciously funding a significant portion of their post-secondary education) and are not indebted to anyone, including credit card companies. Barring tragedy, they do not anticipate owing money to others ever again.

Todd is sincerely looking to make a difference in other's lives, to give back, not only to his children and extended family, but especially to those who are less fortunate so their lives can be impacted in a positive way by his common sense, holistic approach to optimized savings. He regularly prays that his kids enjoy as independent adults someday the same standard of living and financial liberation he and his wife have experienced for quite some time.

"Beyond the Piggy Bank" is his first and perhaps only book. It was written as a lasting legacy to his children so they don't get left behind in the new world order where the American middle class is disappearing at a rapid rate due in part to the unstoppable march of Globalization. He genuinely welcomes your feedback, the good, bad and ugly so he can improve upon this first edition to make it as effective as possible. He is hoping this book will have mass appeal and help educate our nation's youth on broad-based, smart money management practices. (Todd can be reached at Todd_Manning@Outlook.com.)

Author Todd Manning and his wife Caroline enjoying quality time together.

www.ingramcontent.com/pod-product-compliance
Lightning Source LLC
LaVergne TN
LVHW061215060426
835507LV00016B/1941

*9 780990 451129*